M. H Foster, Vere H. Hobart

Report on the Financial Condition of Turkey

M. H Foster, Vere H. Hobart

Report on the Financial Condition of Turkey

ISBN/EAN: 9783337291884

Printed in Europe, USA, Canada, Australia, Japan

Cover: Foto ©Suzi / pixelio.de

More available books at **www.hansebooks.com**

REPORT

ON THE

FINANCIAL CONDITION

OF

TURKEY,

BY

MR. FOSTER AND LORD HOBART,

DATED

DECEMBER 7, 1861.

Presented to both Houses of Parliament by Command of Her Majesty.
1862.

Report on the Financial Condition of Turkey.

Mr. Foster and Lord Hobart to Earl Russell.—(Received December 20.)

My Lord,   *Constantinople, December 7,* 1861.

IN submitting to your Lordship the result of the inquiry with which we were entrusted respecting the condition of the Turkish finances, it seems right that we should notice, in the first place, some peculiar difficulties which have attended that inquiry. Any natural reluctance which the Turkish Government might feel to expose, though for its own advantage, to emissaries of a foreign Government the state of its affairs has not (we believe) been sufficient to prevent it from supplying us, to the best of its ability, with the information necessary for the purposes of our mission. But the difficulty of obtaining, with regard to many of the points to which our attention has been directed, complete and accurate knowledge from official documents, or full explanation, whether written or oral, from persons officially conversant with the subject under consideration; the absence of any sufficiently systematic arrangement or classification of the materials possessed by the Government for forming a judgment respecting its financial position; and the delays, however unintentional, that have taken place in furnishing us with the information which we have actually received,—are causes which have materially impeded our progress, and consumed in mere inquiry time which should have been available for inference and deliberation.

At the outset of our investigation, we thought it desirable to obtain from Her Majesty's Consuls at the principal ports and places of the Empire, and from any other persons whose knowledge and experience might be useful to us, information and opinions as to the operation of the fiscal system of Turkey so far as its effects had come under their observation. We feel bound to express our strong sense of the valuable character of the replies that were furnished to our inquiries, of the ability and industry with which they are drawn up, and of the important assistance which we have derived from them.

With these observations, we have the honour to submit to your Lordship the following Report :—

REVENUE.

The following is a statement of the several sources from which the revenue of Turkey is derived, and of the amount which was received from each source during the Turkish year 1275 (1859-60) :—

No.	Description.					Piastres.	Sterling, converted at 125 piastres per £1.
							£
1	Verghi	..	..	..	..	278,040,021	2,224,320
2	Rachat militaire	..	..	..	..	59,609,119	476,873
3	Dîmes	..	..	..	..	355,564,374	2,844,515
4	Moutons	..	..	..	..	88,291,531	706,332
5	Porcs	..	..	..	..	10,452,473	83,620
6	Douanes de marchandises	..	..	..	..	173,179,783	1,385,438
7	„ de tabac	..	..	..	..	25,727,718	205,822
8	Pêche	..	..	..	..	8,487,253	67,899
9	Contrats	..	..	..	..	2,350,924	18,809
10	Papier timbré	..	..	..	..	3,113,620	24,909

No.	Description.	Piastres.	Sterling, converted at 125 piastres per £1.
			£
11	Boissons	4,690,874	37,527
12	Tapou	6,924,908	55,400
13	Droits divers	101,657,297	813,258
14	Poste	6,267,736	50,142
15	Imprimerie	916,286	7,330
16	Divers immeubles du Gouvernement	3,457,318	27,658
17	Pêcherie	2,003,097	16,020
18	Forêts	660,972	5,288
19	Fermes Impériales	7,810,745	62,486
20	Salines	10,692,175	85,537
21	Mines	1,143,809	9,150
22	Montant des immeubles vendus	505,000	4,040
23	Revenus fixes	46,787,000	374,296
24	Revenu de l'Arsenal	14,839,888	118,719
25	„ du Tidjaret	777,062	6,216
		1,213,950,983	9,711,608

1. *Verghi.*

The " verghi," which produced 278,040,021 piastres, about 2,224,000*l.*, is an impost in the nature of an income tax, and is in theory paid by each individual in proportion to his actual wealth from whatever source derived. But between the " verghi " and an income tax as ordinarily understood there is an important distinction. The latter consists of a fixed annual per-centage on the income of each person liable to the tax, and its total produce, therefore, varies with the aggregate amount of the incomes upon which it is charged. In the case of the " verghi," a fixed annual sum was imposed once for all, many years ago, upon each Province of the Empire, upon each of the districts (" casas ") composing that province, and upon each town or village contained in such district; and the proportion of the sum payable by each individual is decided upon annually by the authorities of the town or village to which he belongs.

The tax as thus assessed and levied gives rise to general and well-founded complaint. There are two great evils incidental to it, viz. :

1. Inequitable apportionment as between provinces, districts, and villages.

It is easily understood that the changes which time has produced in the relative wealth of the different communities have rendered the pressure of a tax fixed upon them at a very distant date unequal in the extreme at the present day. The evil is notorious and admitted on all hands. So great are the inequalities, that while in some villages the impost is scarcely felt, there are some in which it has been so oppressive as to have put a stop to cultivation altogether, and to have driven the population from their homes.

It is evident that this state of things cannot continue to exist without increasing injury to the commercial and industrial interests of the Empire, and to the revenue which depends upon their prosperity.

2. Inequitable apportionment as between individuals.

The amount of " verghi" payable by each person is (as we have already stated) decided annually by the authorities of the town or village to which he belongs. The distribution, which is ostensibly based upon the relative wealth of each member of the community, ascertained, as well as the nature of the case admits, by the produce of his land, the value or rent of his house, mill, or shop, or the scale of his expenditure, has hitherto been made in the rudest, most informal, and most arbitrary manner, without anything like systematic regulation, or any supervision of or check upon the proceedings of the village Councils. The consequence has been that all kinds of unfairness, favouritism, and unjust exaction, have prevailed in the assessment of the impost, and in particular, that the wealthier classes have, by means of their interest with those in official authority, usually escaped with a very light application, or with no application at all, of the tax, which therefore falls with additional weight upon the poorer portion of the community.

Both of these evils have been for a considerable time looked upon by the Turkish Government as extremely serious; and the remedy which it seems inclined to adopt is that of an elaborate census and " cadastre," or valuation of property, and the payment by each individual of a certain fixed per-centage upon his property as thus estimated.

This scheme, or one similar to it in principle, has already been put in force at Smyrna and at Salonica, as well as at Broussa and Janina; and there is (we believe) some intention of adopting it throughout the Empire.

The proposed measure includes the appointment of a Commission of twenty-seven

persons, consisting of a President and twenty-six other members, four of whom are to be
"experts," and which is to be divided into four sections, each of which is to have the
fourth part of a province under its charge, until the whole is completed, and to be assisted
in each town or village by persons chosen by the inhabitants for that purpose.

The Commissioners are to number the population, to measure and value the land, to
value the houses and other property, and to estimate the amount of the incomes derived
from trades, professions, and other sources, in each locality.

This done, a fixed annual per-centage of 4 per mille is to be levied on the value of
all immoveable property ; of 4 per cent. on the proceeds of such property ; and of 3 per
cent. on income proceeding from any other source, such as the profit of trades and professions.

To meet the expense of carrying the measure into effect, a further tax is to be
imposed of 1 per mille on the value of real property, and ½ per cent. on annual income for
one year only.

The measure thus contemplated appears liable to some objections.

A tax paid by the same person both on his capital and his income, both on his
property and that which it produces, must operate in many respects inequitably, and is
sure to be borne with peculiar reluctance. Moreover the scheme is costly, and its cost is
to be defrayed directly by the taxpayer. It effects a change of a somewhat violent
character, and as such would probably be ill-received. Nor is it likely that the difficulties
of a "cadastre," which have been found in France and other European countries insu-
perably great, will be successfully overcome in Turkey. In fact, as regards the localities
in which the scheme has been put in force, we are led to believe that nothing like a fair
measurement or valuation of property has been taken.

On the whole we are disposed to think it may be desirable that some less violent, less
complicated, less tedious, and less costly remedy should be applied to evils which press
urgently for redress, but which for the present seem more susceptible of alleviation than of
absolute cure.

The following scheme (which is in substance nearly the same as one which has been
suggested by a member of the "Conseil du Trésor"), or some modification of it, might
probably be found to be the best of which the nature of the case admits :—

1. With respect to the unequal incidence of the tax upon provinces, casas, and
villages :

The Governor of each province should institute an inquiry with a view to ascertain
what proportion of the amount of "verghi" for which the province is liable should be paid :
(a), by each district (casa) ; (b), by each town or village which belongs to that district.

For this purpose he should call a Council, consisting of Deputies from each casa, and
should decide upon the sum to be paid by each of them, taking into consideration its
population, trade, industry, comparative fertility, and the amount which it pays in the way
of tithe and other taxes.

He should then visit each casa in turn, and call a Council consisting of Deputies
from the different villages of which it is composed, and decide in the same manner upon
the sum to be paid by each village. In his decisions with regard to the villages, he would
of course be assisted by the information and advice of the District Councils.

A full report should be sent by each Governor to the Porte, showing, as clearly as
possible, the data and the principles upon which the re-distribution has been made.

As between the provinces, the re-adjustment of the tax should be made by the Porte
itself, with the help of a Council of Representatives, of whom one should be sent by each
province, and with the further assistance which it might derive from consultation with
former Provincial Governors, and from the results of the inquiries made by the present
Governors in regard to the distribution of the tax.

2. With respect to the unjust apportionment of the tax as between individuals, a
new Regulation has recently been issued by the Porte, with a view to the mitigation of this
evil :

It prescribes a regular course of proceeding for the annual assessment of the tax ;
provides for the making of lists, the keeping of registers, and their conveyance by the
village authorities to the Council of the district, which is to examine and verify them, to
note its approval in the margin, and then to send them back to the Council of the
village.

The District Councils are specially charged to see "that no influential person escape
payment according to his means."

All disputes as to the amount at which any person is rated are to be referred to the
District Council, with an appeal to the superior authorities of the province.

At the end of the year the District Council is to examine the registers, and to compel payment by those who are in default; and to take care that the alleged debts are real, and that the money has not, after being paid, been embezzled by the tax-collector.

The Governors of the Provinces are to superintend the execution of the Regulation, and to make from time to time "personal inspection" in the different towns and villages, to see that it is properly acted upon.

This Regulation, if thoroughly carried into effect, will (there can be no doubt) produce a salutary improvement upon the present system of collection; indeed, we have some reason to think that it has already done so, particularly in regard to the proportion of the tax which is borne by the wealthier classes.

As regards, therefore, the distribution of the tax among individual taxpayers, we think it desirable that the effect of this Regulation should be fairly tried; and that for the present any more ambitious attempt in the same direction might not improbably result in failure.

The Regulation, however, should be amended so as to provide for the fullest publicity being given to the contents of the registers, by requiring that they shall be kept in some easily accessible place, and open, under proper restrictions, to all comers, and, perhaps, that they should be affixed to the doors of the churches, mosques, or other public buildings.

It is most important also that each taxpayer should be able to make himself acquainted as soon as possible with the amount of payment for which he is held liable.

It would, moreover, be desirable that each proprietor should be called upon to make an exact statement in writing of the amount of property held by him, and of its value, subject to penalties for making an incorrect return.

Provision should also be made for receipts being given in every case by the collector to the taxpayers, so that the latter may not be left without the means of legal defence in case of a claim being made upon them for money which they have already paid, and also as affording some degree of additional security against the embezzlement by the collector of any part of the money which he receives.

When the distribution of this impost has been made equitable, and the mode of its assessment and collection improved, it might be found expedient and possible in cases of emergency to raise the revenue of any special year by the temporary imposition of an additional amount of " verghi " in proportion to the amount ordinarily borne by each town or district. This would be no great hardship, for since the contributions were fixed some fifteen years since, the value of money has fallen so considerably that it has, in fact, amounted to a large reduction in the burden of this impost. As the produce of the soil is already heavily taxed, it might be expedient to exempt property paying " dîmes " from any additional impost.

2. Rachat Militaire (Tax for Exemption from Military Service).

The " rachat militaire," of which the proceeds amounted to 59,609,119 piastres, or about 476,000l., is a personal tax levied at the same time and in the same manner as the "verghi," and paid by the non-Mussulman portion of the population, being Ottoman subjects, in consideration of their exemption from military service.

A census was taken for the purposes of this tax about seven years ago, and the amount fixed (as in the case of the " verghi ") which each province, district, and town or village, was to pay: the basis of the assessment being a charge of 5,000 piastres for the exemption of each soldier from service, and the liability of every 180 persons to return one soldier.

The tax is distributed in the same way as the " verghi " among the individuals of each community; and the same complaints are made, and on the same grounds, with regard to its inequitable pressure both on individuals and on communities.

We should hope that as a matter of course the arrangements which have already been made, and those which it is intended to make, for the improved assessment and collection of the "verghi," will be applicable also to the "Rachat Militaire," to the present incidence of which the objections, though inferior in degree, are of a precisely similar kind.

3. Dîmes (Tithes).

Under the name of " dîme " ("uchur ") one-tenth of all the agricultural produce of the country is claimed by the State, which draws from this source a revenue equal to about one-fourth of its whole income; the amount which was received on this account for the year ending March 1860 being, as will be seen, 355,564,374 piastres, or about 2,844,000l.

This tax has hitherto been levied in kind. It has not been taken directly by officers of the Government, but sold to "farmers," who, in conjunction with the local authorities of the different villages, assess the tax upon the cultivators, and collect it on their own account.

The evils of this mode of collection, whether considered with reference to the interests of the revenue or to those of the taxpayer, are, as is generally admitted, extremely great. The "dîmes" of a province are sold to some wholesale contractor by the Government, and the contractor resells them, as it were by retail, for the different districts comprised in the province. A similar retail process is adopted by this second purchaser, so that the "dîme" of a particular village is usually the subject of three or four (sometimes, it is stated, of five or six) different sales before it is finally levied. Thus, between the amount which is due to the Government by the cultivator, and the amount which it receives from the "farmer," there is a margin sufficient to cover several distinct commercial profits. The "dîmes" are also frequently bought by needy speculators, who, in the event of there being loss owing to bad harvests, are unable to meet their engagements, and the debt is added to the amount of arrears. It is evident, therefore, that to the Government the system must be a most expensive one. To the taxpayer, on the other hand, it is injurious in the extreme. In the first place the "farmer" of the tax, having undertaken its collection as a commercial speculation, proceeds, by every means in his power, to enhance its value at the expense of the poorer class of cultivators, whose relative position renders it very difficult, if not impossible, for them to obtain redress for unjust exactions. Of the expedients resorted to by the "farmer" with this object, the most usual appears to be that of collusion with the assessors of the tax (the authorities of the village) to overestimate the amount of produce for which the cultivator is liable, the assessors, of course, participating in the illicit gain. In the next place, the tax being taken in kind, and the cultivator prohibited from selling, or even housing, his produce until it has been assessed to the "dîme," it constantly happens that he is prevented, for a considerable time, or even altogether, from disposing of it; or if bad weather sets in, the grain is subjected to injury from exposure, and the whole loss from this cause is made by the tax-farmers to fall on the cultivator; the delay being occasioned, either by the length of time which is consumed in effecting the different sales of the tax, or (more commonly) by the inability or unwillingness of the "farmer" to make an earlier assessment, or by both these causes combined. Instances even occur (as we are assured), not unfrequently, in which whole crops are allowed to perish uselessly, because they have not been rated to the tithe. In many cases the peasant, being unable to obtain money for his present necessities by the sale of his produce, is driven into the hands of usurers, always to his detriment, and frequently to his ruin. In this manner, also, another convenient instrument of exaction is supplied to the "farmer," of which he frequently avails himself, viz., that of compelling the peasant to pay a sum of money for the early assessment and collection of his tithe.

The necessity of providing some remedy for this state of things has, however, now been recognized by the Porte; and with this view a Regulation has been issued, which is under trial this year in European Turkey, and which it is intended, as we are informed, to apply next year to the rest of the Empire. This Regulation is in substance as follows :—

For the next five years each village is to pay a fixed annual sum to the Government, calculated upon the average annual value of the produce which has been received from it as "dime" during the last five years.

In each village a "Conseil de Dîmes" is to be formed in the spring of each year, presided over in Turkish villages by the Imaum, and in Christian villages by the Curé, and composed of the Muktar (or Mayor) and "notables" and "elders" elected by the inhabitants.

In villages part Mussulman and part Christian, the Conseil is to be composed of the Imaum, Curé, and "notables" and "elders," elected by the Mussulman and Christian inhabitants respectively.

The "Conseil de Dîmes" is to keep a register of the quantity and quality of the different crops produced in the village. It is to take an account from each cultivator, as each kind of produce is harvested in its season, of the sum for which, by approximative calculation, he may appear liable in respect of such produce; and to receive from the producer the amount in five monthly instalments.

When all the produce of the village is harvested, the Council is to send the register in which the amounts so paid on account are to be registered, to the Council of the district, which is to examine it, and in conference with the Village Council, to decide upon the average price of each kind of produce according to the purchases and sales in each village, and the proportion of the whole fixed sum payable by the village for which each cultivator, looking to the amount and market price of his produce, is liable.

The sums paid on account are then to be deducted from the sums charged in the

C

Register against those who have paid them, and the balance is the sum which remains to be paid by the later instalments.

The Muktars of the villages are to to collect the amount, and deposit it in the local Treasury, taking receipts from the Cashier, and receiving for this service a commission of 2½ per cent.

In villages where the "dîme" cannot be paid in money, the Conseil is to take it in kind, and to sell it on account of the village with a view to the payment of the fixed amount of "dîme."

If in any year the fixed amount payable by any village is less than the actual value of its "dîme," the surplus is to be retained by the village, unless the difference is more than one-half the amount of the "dîme," when 10 per cent. extra is to be paid.

If, on the other hand, the actual value of the "dîme" is as much as half less than the fixed amount payable by the village, only the actual value of the "dîme" is to be paid; but the arrears are to be made up in the succeeding years at the rate of 20 per cent. per annum on the fixed amount.

If in any year the crops of a village entirely fail, then on the report of the Governor of the province verifying this loss, it is to be entirely exempt from the tax for that year.

The Council of each district is to make, by means of the registers, a report respecting the produce of each village and its "dîme" account, and to send the report to the Council of the province, which in its turn is to make a similar report, and send it with those of the District Councils to the Central Government.

The estimation which has been made by Government Inspectors for the purposes of this arrangement of the average value of the "dîme" paid during the last five years by each village was obviously a matter of some difficulty, since no official record has been kept of such payments; and the difficulty has been met by taking as the representative of that value, the average annual price given for the "dîme" of each village by the last purchaser of the tax, a course which, inasmuch as the last purchaser must be supposed to have made a profit on the transaction, obviously allows of a certain margin of direct gain to the cultivator. At the end of five years a new assessment will, we presume, be made of the fixed amount payable by each village, so as to give an opportunity for redressing the balance in any case of inequitable apportionment of the tax, either on the first establishment of the new system, or in reference to the changes which may have since occurred in the relative productiveness of the different localities. The registers to be kept by the Conseil des Dîmes of the quantity and quality of the different crops produced in each village will materially facilitate any such assessment.

There can be little doubt that this measure is a very great improvement on the mode of collection which it has replaced. So far, indeed, as the revenue is concerned, it appears that the direct gain to the Treasury will not be so large as might have been hoped for. We are informed by the Finance Minister that, judging from the amount at which the villages have been assessed, the sum received by the Treasury on account of the "dîme" from European Turkey in the present financial year will not exceed by more than 15,000,000 piastres, or about 120,000l., that which was received from it during the past year, when the tax was "farmed;" an increase (supposing that one-half of the total amount of "dîme" is paid by that part of the Empire) of little more than 8 per cent.

To the taxpayer, however, there can be no question but that the change will be productive of immense advantage. He will no longer be the victim of commercial speculation and consequent extortion. He will be able to sell his produce at the time most convenient to him, and will, therefore, cease to be under the necessity either of bribing the "farmer," or of borrowing money at ruinous rates; while the provisions in the new regulation for systematic registration and account will tend to a more equitable distribution of the tax as between the rich and influential members of the community and the peasantry whom they rule.

As regards the actual working of the measure considered as affecting the agricultural classes, the balance of evidence is decidedly in its favour. The replies which we have received from Her Majesty's Consuls and others on this subject are almost unanimous in treating it as a most important and salutary reform. Mr. Consul Suter (of Varna) reports that in his district the change is looked upon as a great boon by the whole population, and states that whereas about 10,000,000 piastres per annum were formerly borrowed of usurers by the peasant farmers in that part of the country, during the present year no more than 4,000,000 piastres have been borrowed by them, the cause of this improvement being that they are now able to sell their produce at their own time. From one or two places there are complaints that too high an amount of payment has been fixed, as the last five years include a period of war prices, and also of the severity with which the new assessment has been enforced. Others aver that the poorer cultivators suffer because, being unable to wait for a market, they are compelled to sell their produce immediately after harvest, when prices are at the very lowest, whereas the amount of the "dîme" is calculated at an average price. But these complaints, even supposing them to be genuine, are exceptional, and do not seriously diminish the general prospect of success.

It has been objected to the substitution of payments in money for those in kind, that in many parts of the interior the cultivators have no market for their produce and can only obtain currency at a ruinous loss. It will be observed that the regulation contains a provision which is intended to meet this difficulty; the opinions, however, which we have collected with regard to it do not lead us to suppose that the objection is one of serious importance. Whatever may be its force, it applies equally to the "verghi," which is paid in currency. It may be hoped also that some effort will soon be made to supply the great want of the country—that of roads, the absence of which, in many districts, alone denies a market to agricultural industry. It seems at least unadvisable to legislate on the supposition that a defect so serious and anomalous will never be remedied.

On the whole then, the new measure, while producing a direct increase of revenue of no inconsiderable amount, will (as may fairly be anticipated) contribute in a very important degree to increase it indirectly by the relief which it will give to the cultivators of the soil, and the consequent stimulus to production and trade throughout the Empire.

Comparing it again with other measures of direct collection which naturally suggest themselves, we are inclined to prefer that which has actually been adopted.

Direct collection by Government officers unconnected with the inhabitants of the district would have been more expensive as well as less acceptable to the population; while in requiring a fixed amount from each village and making the village itself responsible for its assessment and collection there is this obvious advantage, that the blame of an inequitable distribution or unjust collection falls not on the Government, but on the village itself, which elects its own assessors and collectors.

Again, collection in kind rather than in money would, if made directly by the Government, in the first place be injurious to it on account of the extreme uncertainty which it would involve as to the probable amount of the receipts from the tax; and in the next place, would imply the assumption by the Government of commercial functions, which it can never conveniently or profitably exercise.

While, however, approving in substance of the new regulation we think it susceptible of improvement in detail.

It is most important, for instance, that provision should be made for the free access of each cultivator to the register, so that he may ascertain at once the sum for which he is held liable and the state of his account, and may also assure himself that he is duly credited with all that he has paid.

For this purpose it seems desirable, as in the case of the "verghi," that the register should be kept in some easily accessible place, and open under proper regulation to general inspection: and perhaps also that lists taken from the register should be affixed to the churches, mosques, and other public buildings, a practice which (as we understand) would be in accordance with popular usage in this country.

In this regulation, as in that respecting the "verghi," no provision is made for compelling the Muktar to give receipts to the taxpayers. This is a serious defect which should be promptly remedied.

4. *Sheep.*

The tax on sheep produced in the year ending 1859–60 was 88,291,531 piastres, or about 706,000*l.*, and was estimated at somewhat less for the following year. It was formerly a mere tithe in kind, one sheep in every ten being taken by the State; at present it is a money payment supposed to represent about a-tenth of the estimated annual value; its average rate is for some districts about 4 piastres, and for others about 2 piastres per sheep.

This tax is "farmed," and so far as that portion of it is concerned which is levied on nomad flocks, such as those of Albania and a great part of Anatolia, the absence of any effectual means of checking or controlling direct collection may render it difficult for the Government to dispense with the services of the "farmer," unless arrangements were entered into with the Chiefs of tribes under which the tax could be compounded for by a fixed annual payment. In cultivated districts, where the flocks are more settled, there seems no reason why direct collection, desirable on so many accounts both for the interests of the revenue and the taxpayer, should not be adopted.

5. *Pigs.*

The duty on pigs, which yielded 10,452,473 piastres, or about 83,000*l.*, was before the ___ 1852, 3 piastres per head; in that year it was raised to 10 piastres per head, a rate which seems, in some important districts at least, to have seriously diminished the supply. Mr. Consul Blunt of Philippopolis, and Mr. Consul Wilkinson of Salonica, both speak in strong terms of the injurious effect of this tax, at its present rate, on the Christian peasantry throughout European Turkey. Mr. Blunt remarks that, " if the peasant treats himself to meat twenty times a-year, on fifteen of those occasions he uses pork ; and that the pig is an economical and necessary member in the peasant's cottage." He states that in consequence of the high rate of duty the number of pigs in Roumelia has, it is calculated, decreased by 60 per cent. ; that at Philippopolis there were 30,000 pigs in 1857, and not more than 13,000 in 1860 ; and at Nisch in 1857 about 40,000 pigs, whereas at present there are not more than 17,000.

It is obvious that if this be the state of the case, any small gain which the Treasury may derive from the increased duty is purchased at an extravagant cost of suffering to the agricultural population ; and that a reduction of this tax, while involving a direct fiscal loss of very trifling amount, would not only be a great relief to the peasants of Roumelia, but would indirectly benefit the public revenue by improving their condition.

The taxation of pigs should commence, not as at present at the age of three months, but at a later period. The disproportion of the tax to the value at so early an age is (it is stated) such as frequently to cause the destruction of the animal to escape payment of the tax.

There seems no reason why the vicious system of " farming," which is in the course of abolition with respect to other branches of the revenue, should not be abolished also in the case of this tax.

6. Customs.

The Customs duties produced in 1859-60 a gross amount of 173,179,783 piastres, or about 1,385,000l. They have hitherto been farmed at all the ports of the Empire except Constantinople, and certain ports in the Sea of Marmora, the Dardanelles, and on the Asiatic coasts of the Black Sea, which are dependent upon the Custom-house of the capital, and even at these places until quite recently, as regards some classes of goods. They consist of—

1. A duty of 3 per cent. ad valorem on importation, and a duty of 2 per cent. ad valorem on actual sale of the imported goods; in all, an import duty of 5 per cent. ad valorem.

2. An export duty of 12 per cent. ad valorem : viz., 9 per cent. on goods when entering the port of export from any other port or place in Turkey ; and 3 per cent. when shipped for exportation, whether to a port of Turkey or of any foreign country.

The duty of 9 per cent. is, it appears, also charged on goods in the interior when removed from one town or district to another. The Consul at Diarbekir states that internal traffic between towns even one mile apart pays this high Customs duty.

3. A duty of 3 per cent. ad valorem on goods in transit.

In pursuance of Treaties which have recently been concluded with certain foreign Powers, these duties are to be altered, and are in future to be as follows :—

1. An import duty of 8 per cent. ad valorem, taken once for all at the place and time of importation.

2. An export duty of 8 per cent. ad valorem for the first year, diminishing each succeeding year by 1 per cent. until it becomes a duty of 1 per cent., at which point it is to remain.

3. A transit duty of 2 per cent. (instead of the present 3 per cent.), which after eight years is to be reduced to 1 per cent.*

Tobacco and salt are exempted from these stipulations, and in return the export duty on the former is to be abolished at once.

A Table, drawn up, so far as regards foreign countries other than England, from official Returns which were obtained at our request from the different foreign Embassies at Constantinople, shows the total exports and imports of Turkey in the year 1859 to and from the countries which it enumerates, and which include nearly all those with which Turkey carries on any important trade. The gross amount of revenue which at the rates of duty now in force ought to have been received upon this amount of traffic was found to be 2,069,200l. The actual gross amount of revenue derived from Customs duties in Turkey for the year 1859 was 1,410,580l. Supposing, therefore, that the Table referred to comprised the whole of the trade which is subject to Customs duties in Turkey, the produce of those duties was in the year 1859 less by 658,620l. than it would have been under a perfectly efficient system of collection. The deficiency, however, must, in

---

* The conversion of these ad valorem rates into specific duties on goods is confided to Tariff Commissions, which include the Representatives of the different foreign nations concerned.

reality, have been considerably greater, since there must be added to the sum above given as that which ought to have been received in Customs duties upon the traffic comprised in the Table, the amount of duty payable on the trade of those countries trading with Turkey which are not comprised in it: the amount payable on the traffic from port to port of Turkey (which is also subject to the export duty of 12 per cent.), the duty of 9 per cent. on a portion of the trade of the interior, and the produce of the duties on goods in transit.

This important deficiency in the receipts from Customs duties may, we think, be attributed chiefly to the following causes:—

1. The system of "farming," which is generally admitted to be ruinous to the Exchequer.

2. The ease with which the duty of 2 per cent. payable on actual sale is evaded.

3. The absence of precautions to prevent goods imported for consumption from being passed as goods in transit, and so escaping at the lower duty.

4. Defects in the regulations under which the duties are collected.

1 and 2. The two former of these causes will now be removed.

Direct collection has been established at Constantinople, and is in the course of being established throughout the country. Great as may be the losses of the Government occasioned by dishonest collectors, we cannot believe that they will be sufficient to counterbalance those which it suffers from the monopoly prices and frequent defalcations of the " farmers " of Customs duties. The system of " farming " is inherently and necessarily vicious; the defects of direct collection depend upon those of the human character, which are susceptible of cure.

3. The adoption of measures to ensure that goods intended for consumption in the country shall not pay duty as goods in transit is urgently required; the more so, as under the new Treaties the difference between the import and the transit duties will be considerably greater than it has hitherto been. At present there appears to be no check in this respect, except the mere declaration of the importing merchant. Either the duties ought to be taken at the port of arrival on all goods whether for transit or sale in the country, and a drawback given on them at the place of re-export, or bond should be given by the importing merchant for their being sent out of the country by way of some specified port or place within a certain time.

4. Defects in the regulations under which the duties are collected.

In this respect an important change will be made under the new Treaties. Attempts at fraud or smuggling, on the part of the importers or exporters, are now punishable only by the exaction of double duty. In future they will be punishable by confiscation of the goods.

Under the present system, when neighbouring Custom-houses are let to different farmers, a competition arises between them, and as each endeavours to attract goods to the port which he farms, merchants are induced to pay the duties at the port at which they can obtain the greatest abatement from the just amount of duty. This loss of duty apparently falls on the farmer of the revenue, but as he of course calculates upon those reductions in the price which he pays to the Government, the loss in reality falls upon the public Treasury. These private arrangements are detrimental to fair trade between merchants; and it not unfrequently happens that the revenue farmer himself acts as a merchant, and by passing his own goods without duty, while he exacts the full amount of duty from others, is enabled to appropriate to himself the monopoly of the trade in certain articles. These evils will cease when the system of direct collection has been put in force.

We have carefully examined the system of collection at the chief Custom-house at Constantinople, and witnessed the mode of passing the goods, and of keeping the accounts.

In regard to the mode of passing the goods, some changes appear to be required.

An examiner opens the bales of goods, and proclaims their nature and weight or quantity to a clerk who is at hand, and who enters these particulars in a book. Both these functionaries are very ill paid, and there is little to prevent the examiners from making a false statement as to the goods at the instance of the merchant's agent, or, if he makes a true one, the clerk from making a false entry. We think that these officers should in future be better paid, so as to ensure their being taken from a higher class of society.

The manner of keeping the accounts at the Custom-house will be noticed in that part of our Report which relates to the subject of accounts generally.

Two important checks upon fraud on the part of importers, which are usual in other countries, are dispensed with at the Turkish Custom-house, viz., the production of the ship's manifest to the Custom officers, and the delivery at the Custom-house by the importer of a detailed statement of the nature, quantity, and quality of the goods imported. The first is valuable for the purpose of ensuring that the whole cargo of the vessel is brought to the Custom-house, and that no part of it has been illegally landed: the second, which is the more important, chiefly as affording a certain degree of security against misrepresentation by the examining and registering officers of the quantity or quality of the goods.

In cases where the value placed by importers upon goods liable to duty appears to the authorities at the Custom-house to be too low, they should have the power of taking possession of the goods on paying the owner a price from 10 to 20 per cent. above the value at which they were declared.

The Custom-houses at the outports should be subjected to periodical inspection by a superior officer selected for the purpose from the chief office at the capital, and it would be found a useful check to transfer the officials from time to time from one port to another.

Means should also be taken for making as public as possible the rates under the new tariff when they have been fixed, and tables of the rates at which foreign coins are accepted should be conspicuously placed at each Custom-house as a check upon the abuses to which the deficiency of the Turkish currency gives rise.

The changes which we have thus suggested, together with those to which we have referred as having been already adopted, will, we trust, have the effect of greatly diminishing the difference between the amount legally payable and the amount actually paid in Customs duties.

It remains to consider what will be the effect on the revenue of the changes about to be effected by the new Treaties.

The immediate reduction of the export duties by 4 per cent. (from 12 to 8) is compensated by an increase of only 3 per cent. on the import duties. Any loss, however, which may be thus occasioned, is likely (we think) to be at least supplied by the substitution of an import duty, taken once for all, for the former more complicated arrangement, under which the 2 per cent. chargeable on actual sale was frequently evaded. So frequent, indeed, does the evasion seem to have been, that the new 8 per cent. import duty might fairly be considered to have been substituted for a duty, not of 5, but of 3 per cent.

In the first year or two, therefore, we do not anticipate any loss to the revenue from the new arrangement, though it includes the reduction from 3 to 2 per cent. of the transit duty.

The reduction of the export duties at the rate of 1 per cent. per annum, until at the end of eight years only a nominal duty is levied, must considerably affect the revenue obtained from Customs; but the relief and impulse which it cannot fail to give to agriculture and commerce, especially to the former, upon which a very large proportion of the burden of taxation is at present thrown, may be expected to result in a general increase in the revenue derived from other taxes, more particularly in that which is the chief fiscal resource of the country, the "dîme." In this general improvement the receipts from Customs duties will, of course, participate, so that the falling off, even in this respect, will not be so great as might at first sight be supposed.

On the whole, then. we think that under the head of Customs duties no serious decrease of receipts need be anticipated, since the effect of the improvements in the mode of collection which have already been adopted, and of those which we trust will be adopted in accordance with the suggestions which we have made, may be set against the diminution which might be expected to result from the gradual abolition, considered by itself, of the export duties. That the changes which have been made in regard to these duties must tend greatly to improve the general condition of the public treasury, there can be little doubt.

The non-existence in Turkish ports of bonded warehouses in which goods may be stored for re-exportation without payment of duty, or, if intended for home consumption, without payment of duty until they are taken out of the warehouse, is a serious disadvantage to the commerce, and therefore to the revenue, of Turkey. The erection of such warehouses would increase the public revenue directly, by increasing the receipts from Customs duties, since the facilities which it would give to the merchant for selling his goods for consumption in the country at the time which the state of the market might render most convenient and most profitable, would diminish the price, and therefore increase the quantity of imported goods; and it would have a similar effect indirectly, since the increase of shipping and commerce which it would attract to them would materially add to the wealth and importance of the ports of Turkey, and especially of Constantinople, singularly adapted as it is, by natural advantages, for the purposes of a great commercial entrepôt.

7. *Duty on Tobacco.*

The excise duty on tobacco produced 25,727,718 piastres, or about 205,000*l.*

This tax is farmed, and is levied on the *ad valorem* principle, as follows :—

Value per Oke.	Duty.
Below 7½ piastres	1½ piastres.
7½ to 15 ,, ...	3 ,,
Above 15 ,, ...	6 ,,

The duty is taken by the farmer of the tax (as stated in the Government regulation) "on the purchase of the tobacco by tradesmen or merchants for the purpose of being sold in shops or warehouses."

With respect to this tax, the remark is obvious, that in a country containing a population of 25,000,000 at the least, and in which most men, and a great many women, smoke incessantly, 205,000*l.* is a very small sum to derive from an article which in England, France, and other European countries yields millions to the Treasury, and which is universally recognized as one of the very fittest subjects for taxation.

It must be remembered, however, that in Turkey there is no possible mode of drawing any large revenue from the home consumption of this article, but by means of a monopoly or an internal duty, since the tobacco consumed in Turkey is chiefly of native growth. Moreover, a monopoly, which has proved so costly and difficult of enforcement in European countries, would probably fail altogether in Turkey from the want of efficient executive arrangements ; while an Excise duty levied directly upon the producer, and not confined (as is actually the case) to the purchase of the article by the dealer, would be objectionable not only on account of the difficulty of collection, but of the serious check which it would give to production.

It would, of course, be possible to increase the present excise duties on tobacco, which (as will be observed) are fixed at a rate far below that which has been adopted in countries where tobacco is a principal fiscal resource, and which amounts to several hundreds per cent. on the value. But it is not likely that a rate of duty at all approaching to that amount would be successful in Turkey against illicit trading, unless under a far more efficient system of collection than that which is at present in force. The production of tobacco in the Empire has generally been estimated at not less than 30,000,000 okes, and as the revenue derived from it is less than 26,000,000 piastres, an average duty is shown of less than 1 piastre per oke. As the present Tariff ranges from 1½ to 6 piastres per oke, it is evident that there must be a large evasion of the tax.

There can, however, be no reason why the mode of collection should not be revised with a view to render it more efficient, or why its efficiency should not be so far increased as to admit of a very large addition to the present impost on tobacco, and to the revenue derived from it. For this purpose it would be absolutely necessary to abolish the "farming" system, and to substitute for it direct collection by the officers of the Government. The Assessor and Collector should be different persons, so that the one might act as a check upon the proceedings of the other ; and special Inspectors should be appointed — selected for their honesty, and paid so as to preserve it—to watch over the collection of the tax. There could be no more useful employment for the "Conseil du Trésor," or other financial advisers of the Porte, than the preparation of a measure of this nature, and the careful observation of its results.

In the meantime, and even under the present imperfect regulations for collection, the rates of duty might (as it appears to us) be to some extent increased, not only without any countervailing decrease of consumption, but without any serious diminution of revenue from fraudulent evasion of the tax. In particular there seems no reason why the scale should abruptly close at the comparatively low price of 15 piastres per oke, thus subjecting the tobaccos of a higher value, which vary in price up to a maximum of about 100 piastres the oke, to the same rate of duty.

Revision is also required in the Tariff as it now exists with regard to the classes in which the several qualities of tobacco are placed. For instance, that called "taireh," which now is worth 60 piastres at the place of growth, remains in the lowest class, and pays only the smallest rate of duty.

We propose that the following scale of duties should be substituted for those at present in force :—

Value per Oke.	Duty.	Value per Oke.	Duty.
Below 7½ piastres	2 piastres.	25 to 40 piastres	15 piastres.
7½ to 15 ,, ...	4 ,,	40 piastres and upwards	25 ,,
15 to 25 ,, ...	10 ,,		

When the machinery of collection has been reconstructed and invigorated, a further increase of duty might be tried. The only objection to such a course would consist in the degree of probability which might exist of its serious unpopularity, and which may render it necessary that the measures taken for increasing the duty should be gradual and tentative in their character.

8. *Duty on Fish.*

This tax produced 8,487,253 piastres, or about 67,000*l.* The duty on fish is 20 per cent. *ad valorem*; but, in addition to this, there is among the "droits divers" of some localities a duty of 50 per cent. on "taglians," or fishing implements. Mr. Consul Finn states that in some places "the (Revenue) Officers take two fishes out of three." Such an impost must act as a serious discouragement to this branch of industry, and might probably be reduced with direct advantage to the interests even of the revenue. In Chio the duty is stated to be 25 per cent. At Bagdad the river fisheries pay 50 per cent. It seems desirable that these duties should be revised, with a view not only to their reduction, but to the establishment of uniform rates for all parts of the empire.

9. *Contracts.*

This is a duty of 2½ per cent. on the registration of leases of houses, such registration being by law compulsory. It produces the small sum of 2,350,924 piastres, or about 18,000*l.*, which might certainly be greatly increased if a more effective regulation were adopted for enforcing the law.

At present the person making a contract is bound to register it at the police-office, but this process is frequently dispensed with, especially by influential proprietors who are not afraid of a too rigorous inquiry into their proceedings. An important improvement would be to deprive of legal validity all contracts which were not duly registered as required by law.

10. *Stamp Duties.*

The amount received on account of stamps was 3,113,620 piastres, or about 25,000*l.*; a very small sum to derive from a source which in England and in France yields annually several millions sterling. Very few documents are subject to stamp duty in Turkey. Money bonds, which pay a tax of 1 per mille; title-deeds, conveyances, leases, and other papers connected with the transfer of real property, which pay a uniform duty of 5 piastres each, are, as we are informed, the only classes of documents to which this duty is applied. Moreover, unstamped documents belonging to these classes are, it appears, in practice at least, treated as legally valid by the judicial authorities; and no sufficient provision is made for supplying the different districts with stamped paper.

We believe that the attention of the Turkish Government has been recently directed to this subject, and it is most desirable that steps should be taken without delay to extend the incidence and increase the productiveness of this tax. Receipts, checks upon bankers, bills of exchange, promissory notes, and mercantile paper in general, should be subjected to a stamp duty proportionate, so far as is consistent with convenience of collection, to the value for which they are drawn; and the duty now existing on title-deeds and other papers relating to the transfer or tenancy of real property which, as we have stated, is only 5 piastres, should be considerably increased according to an *ad valorem* scale.

The legal invalidity of unstamped documents of a class to which stamps are applicable by law should be assured, as far as is possible, by a new and stringent enactment, and by strict injunctions to the authorities throughout the Empire.

It is also very important that, besides stamped paper, adhesive stamps should be issued and made readily procurable by the public both in the capital and in the provinces. The additional facility which would thus be given for a compliance with the law would be such as would, in all probability, make a very important difference in favour of the Treasury as regards the receipts from this branch of revenue.

11. *Excise on Alcoholic Liquors.*

In the year ending March 1860 the receipts from this source were 4,690,874 piastres, or about 37,000*l.*, the duty having been at that time 10 per cent. on the value of all such liquors.* For the following year it was resolved to raise the duty to 20 per cent., but the result was not an increase but a diminution of revenue so great that it became necesary to return to the original rate of 10 per cent., which is that now in force.

---

* The duty is levied at the place where the liquor is manufactured, and is charged on the alcohol which is taken in for that purpose; a certain fixed proportion being assumed as that which the alcohol bears to the manufactured liquor.

It seems probable that this falling off in the revenue was caused by the advantage given to liquors imported from abroad as against those manufactured in the country, by the additional duty placed upon the latter, while the duty on the former remained at its Treaty rate of 5 per cent. *ad valorem.* It would seem that spirituous liquors ought to have been among the articles exempted from the fetters imposed upon the fiscal policy of Turkey by her Commercial Treaties. But however unrestricted she might be in regard to the taxation of this article, the revenue drawn from it in Turkey could not (as it would appear) be otherwise than trifling when compared with that derived from the same source in other countries. In Turkey (so far as we can learn) the bulk of the population, the inhabitants of the interior, are not consumers of spirituous liquors. It is only in the few large and populous towns, which are, for the most part, sea-ports, that there is any appreciable demand for them. It seems scarcely just, however, that the Turkish Government should be precluded by engagements with foreign Powers from availing itself of any change for the worse which may take place in the habits of the people, and, whether such change should take place or not, from using to the best advantage this deservedly favourite instrument of taxation.

12. *Tapou (Registration).*

The source of revenue bearing this title is a registration fee of 2½ per cent. on the transfer of a certain description of landed property which lapses to the State in default of direct heirs of the owner, and 5 per cent. on the grant of titles to the holder of such property.

It produced, in the year 1859-60, 6,924,908 piastres, or about 55,000*l.*, but credit is taken for more than double that sum in the following year, on the ground (we believe) that more stringent measures had been adopted for the collection of the tax.

We are informed that the aggregate amount of property held under "tapou" titles is very large, and it seems deserving of consideration whether it would not be desirable to allow of the conversion of this property into freehold, on condition of a certain yearly contribution or a sum once for all payable by the holder to the State. It seems probable that the revenue would greatly profit by such an arrangement, and it is certain that a freehold tenure of property is more conducive to the general prosperity than a precarious tenure such as that under which these lands are held.

13. *Miscellaneous Duties.*

The "droits divers," which produced 101,657,297 piastres, or about 813,000*l.*, are excessively numerous. Among them is a duty of 2½ per cent. *on every article of native manufacture sold in shops,* a duty on the shops themselves, on workmen, on the sale of cattle and horses, on goods sold by auction, on fairs, on pastures, on sheep-folds, on weighing articles by a Government officer, on mills, on licenses to sell shot, on agricultural produce and other goods entering a town; and a duty called "derbend," which is a toll levied on merchandize other than foreign, at frequent intervals on the mountain-pass or other substitute for a road along which the goods are conveyed. Many more might be enumerated; but the taxes imposed under this head are different for different localities, so that an article or branch of trade subject to a particular tax in one place would not be subject to it in another.

The information which we have received leads us to believe that these duties are, as might be expected, extremely burdensome; their multiplicity is indeed in itself sufficient to give them this character. Even if they were collected directly by officers of the Government, the incessant interference of the tax-gatherer which they imply would be difficult to support; as it is, the objections to them are aggravated by their surrender to "farmers," whose gains are proportionate to the success of their exactions.

We trust that the Turkish Government will without delay direct its attention to these duties, with a view to their careful and complete revision. The abolition of any among them of which the produce, either singly or in the aggregate, is considerable, might be undesirable in the present critical condition of the National Exchequer; but it is obvious that there must be some of them of which the amount received by the Treasury is so small as not to be worth the expense of collection combined with the annoyance which it causes to the people, and others of which the amount, though in itself not inconsiderable, is so detrimental to production and trade as ultimately and on the whole to be injurious to the fiscal interests of the country. To the latter class would probably be found to belong the "derbend," or toll on merchandise mentioned above, and of which great complaints are made; the monopoly of dyeing and ironing manufactured goods, which is stated to be the cause of serious injury to them; and the duties on agricultural produce entering a town,

D

forming as they do a serious addition to the share, already disproportionate, borne by the produce of the land in the taxation of the country.

The 2½ per cent. on all goods whatever of native manufacture sold in shops seems to be an impost of the worst kind, and one of which the abolition, as soon as the financial condition of the country would bear the immediate loss, could not fail so to benefit commerce as to produce a large ultimate increase of the general revenue.

It may be hoped also that it will be found possible, when these duties are revised and their number abridged, to collect them directly with advantage to the revenue. The injury to the taxpayer caused by the farming of these taxes is proportionate to their number.

A portion of the proceeds of these duties was formerly retained in each of the districts where they are paid, for the purpose of defraying its municipal expenses; at present the whole amount is paid into the public Exchequer, on the understanding that the Government will itself provide funds for any necessary municipal expenditure. The consequence, inevitable perhaps in the present instance, owing to the pecuniary difficulties of the Government, has been that towns and districts have been obliged to forego altogether many of the local improvements and arrangements nécessary for their welfare.

It is, we think, very important that a fund should be specially set apart for the local requirements of each district, and desirable also that such a fund should be supplied by contributions from the district itself. And with this view we would suggest that when (as we trust will at no distant time be the case) the Government shall find itself in a position to dispense with a considerable portion of these miscellaneous taxes, some one simple and uniform tax, such as a house-tax, should be imposed in their stead, and its proceeds devoted entirely to local purposes.

14. *Post Office.*

The sum received from this source was 6,267,736 piastres, or about 50,000l. The expense of administration appears in the Accounts of the Minister of Finance under the head of "Entretien des relais et frais d'administration des Postes," as 9,220,695 piastres, or about 73,000l. It appears, however, that these "relais" are used by the Government not only for postal but for other purposes, and that in reality there is some small gain to the State on account of this service.

Scarcely any approach to an efficient postal system has hitherto been made by the Turkish Government. The communication with foreign countries and between the ports of Turkey is in great part carried on by the steamers of independent foreign companies, of which any one who pleases may avail himself. Each of these Companies has its own separate post office, and neither from these offices nor from those of the Government are any letters delivered except upon application on the part of those to whom they are addressed.

As regards the interior of the country all carrying of letters except by the Government is illegal, but so long as the state of the roads compels a high rate of postage it is not likely that the prohibition will be much regarded.

Constantinople and its environs are, as regards their internal correspondence, entirely without any regular postal arrangements.

A well-organised postal service, monopolized by the Government, has been looked upon by most States as an advantage to the public interests generally, as well as a convenient means of adding to the national revenue; and we would recommend this subject to the early and careful attention of the Turkish Government. In particular, there seems no reason why the great advantages, which are so well understood by other States, of collection by means of postage stamps should not be extended to this country. Even on the supposition, which it is to be hoped has no prospect of realization, that no improvement were to take place in the means of internal communication, some considerable direct gain to the Treasury must result from the establishment of an efficient system of postage, while its effect upon the National Exchequer would probably be felt still more beneficially in the increase of general revenue which would be consequent on the commercial and other advantages of such a measure.

15. *The Government Printing Office.*

Under this head appears a sum of 916,286 piastres (about 7,000l.), being the proceeds of the sale of Government journals, printed laws or regulations, and other papers issued by the Government.

16. *Miscellaneous and Real Property belonging to the State.*

This resource, which produced a sum of 3,457,318 piastres (about 27,000l.), consists of the rent of various buildings, such as houses or mills, belonging to the Government.

Much of this property might probably be sold with great advantage to the State, especially if the exclusion of foreigners from proprietary rights in Turkey were, as it ought to be, abolished.   Where the property is retained by the Government, the leases, which, we believe, are now annual, should be for longer periods, and care should be taken in every case thoroughly to advertise the property for which a tenant is required.

17. *Fisheries.*

The sum received from this source, 2,003,097 piastres, or about 16,000*l.*, consists of the rent derived from the fisheries belonging to the State, which are, we believe, for the most part leased annually to private persons.   It can scarcely be supposed that this sum represents anything like the largest amount which might easily be derived from this branch of revenue.   If lists were annually made and published as widely as possible of the fisheries to be leased and of the terms on which they would be let, so as to throw them fairly open to public competition, considerable improvement might be expected in the receipts on this account.   Probably, also, if leases were granted for longer periods, a better price would be given for them in the market, and more care be taken by their holders to preserve and foster the fisheries in which they were interested.

18. *Forests.*

The forests of Turkey, which are, we believe, almost exclusively the property of the Government, produce 660.972 piastres, or no more than 5,000*l.* per annum.

In Greece, which is in extent scarcely one-fifth of European Turkey, and which, though some parts of it produce timber of considerable value, is renowned in about an equal degree for the sterility of its soil and the inefficiency of its administration, the forests are estimated to yield annually to the Government 270,000 francs, or 10,800*l.*

We trust that the attention of the Turkish Government, which was so far roused some two years since upon this subject as to cause the preparation of a law with regard to it which has never been carried into effect, may now be directed in earnest to the utilisation of the national forests, which are admitted on all hands to be of great value.   What is required seems to be simply that the Porte should lay aside all jealousy of private enterprize, whether national or foreign, and turn its forests to the best advantage by throwing them open to the freeest competition of individuals and companies, taking care of course in each case that a fair per-centage on the profits of the undertaking is secured for the public revenue.

It may be hoped that no long time will elapse before the value of the forests of Turkey is further enhanced by the all-important construction of roads, without which, indeed, it must be admitted that they can never be expected to yield to the State an amount at all proportionate to their real value.

19. *Farms belonging to the State.*

These produced a sum of 7,810,745 piastres, or about 62,000*l.*   These farms are held under annual leases, and the amount which they yield is (as we are assured) far below their real value.   It is probable that the best mode of turning them to advantage would be to sell them, to which there may be in many cases objections of a political nature.   The next best mode would be to let them under long leases, so as to give the cultivator some interest in the soil, and to induce him to husband instead of waste its resources.   In this case the importance of allowing foreigners to hold property in freehold or on long leases becomes again evident.   It is by foreign capital that the land would be made most valuable both to the Government which would receive a higher price for the property, and to the community which would profit by the development of its productive power.

20. *Salt Works.*

The sale of salt, the produce of Government works, yielded 10,692,175 piastres, or about 85,000*l.*   Hitherto these works have been "farmed," and the proceeds sold by the farmer to the public at a price fixed by the Government.   The Porte has now (as we believe) taken the monopoly into its own hands, and there is little doubt that the revenue will profit by the change.

As salt is excepted in the new Treaties from the stipulations respecting Customs duties and prohibitions, it may be inferred that the Turkish Government has had some intention of making use of the monopoly of this article for the purpose of increasing the revenue.   All the salt now consumed in Turkey is (as we are informed) of native produc-

the monopoly price now taken by the Government, and to prohibit, or to place a prohibitive duty upon the importation of the article. It does not appear, however, that there is any present intention of adopting this course, which is one to which much valid objection may be taken. It is evident from the smallness of the sum now received by the Government on this account, that in order to obtain anything like a considerable revenue from salt, it would be necessary to increase the monopoly price to an extent which would scarcely fail to create general dissatisfaction. Unless in case of the strongest fiscal necessity, a novel impost, enhancing very seriously the cost of one of the prime necessaries of life, does not appear desirable.

21. *Mines.*

The mines of Greece produce annually about 20,000*l.* (500,000 francs) to the State ; those of Turkey only about 9,000*l.* : facts which are conclusive as to the use which has hitherto been made of the rich mineral resources at the disposal of the Turkish Government. A new code of regulations respecting mines has, however, recently been issued, evidently with the object of turning the mines of the country to a more profitable account.

These regulations provide for the issue of State licenses (or concessions) for the working of mines under certain restrictions and conditions, and under the superintendence of a central " Council of Mines," which is to appoint inspectors to see that the restrictions are observed and the conditions fulfilled. Any person may search for a mine on his own property, but no one on the property of another person or of the State without a regular authority from the Government, and no person may work a mine without a direct license or commission from the State, which is to receive a rent proportionate to the richness of the mine. These concessions can only be granted to Turkish subjects ; but subjects of foreign States may be shareholders in any concessionary Company. No concession is to be granted unless it be proved by documentary evidence to the satisfaction of the Government that the undertaking is likely to be profitable, that the capital is sufficient, and that the mine will be worked in the " manner which offers the most facilities." No concessionary can increase the capital which he employs upon the mine without the authority of the Government ; and if in the working of the mine a metal different to that for which the concession was granted is discovered, the working of the mine must cease until a new concession is obtained. The regulations go further still, and actually subject smelting operations throughout the Empire to very similar restrictions.

Confronted with such an array of difficulties and delays, it is not likely that capital will venture freely upon the field of Turkish mining enterprise. As regards the working of mines on property belonging to the Government, some of these regulations are, no doubt, necessary or expedient with a view to the due protection of such property ; but others are useless and mischievous. In particular the implied refusal to allow foreigners or foreign Companies to become concessionaries must seriously detract from the prospect of profit to be drawn from these mines.

With regard to mines on private property, the system adopted in England and other countries of leaving such mines entirely at the disposal of the owner of the property, and free from any fiscal interference or impost whatever, is that which appears most conducive to the prosperity of a nation, and therefore in the long run to its fiscal interests. Supposing, however, that the Turkish Government is not prepared to adopt such a system, but will continue to treat the mines of the whole country as the property of the Government, the course which it ought to take seems to be to allow any person whatever, or any Company however composed, to search for or work the mines upon private property without any restriction or condition whatever but the consent of the owner of the property, each such mine being subjected to an annual contribution to the State proportionate to its value.

22. *Sales of Real Property.*

The sale of real property belonging to the State produced the sum of 505,000 piastres, or about 4,000*l.* The question of the sale of State property as a fiscal expedient deserves (as we have already remarked), and seems likely to receive, the attention of the Government.

23. *Fixed Revenues.*

These, which amount to 46,787,000 piastres, or about 374,000*l.*, are the fixed sums

24 and 25. *Revenues of the Arsenal and of the Tidjaret.*

Under these heads are sums of 14,839,888 piastres (or about 118,000*l.*) and 777,062 piastres (or about 6,000*l.*) respectively, which include the tolls of the bridge at Galata, the light-house dues, and a portion of the dues on workmen and trading corporations. These are the only Departments of the Government enjoying the mischievous privilege of special revenues.

If the suggestions which we have made on this subject in another portion of our Report are attended to, the whole of the public revenues, without exception, will in future be paid to the Receiver-General, and carried to the general account.

EXPENDITURE.

The following is an abstract of the Budget of Expenditure for the Turkish year 1275 (1859-60):—

No.	Description.	Piastres.	Sterling converted at 125 piastres per £1.
1	Foreign debt, interest, and sinking fund	111,377,890	891,023
2	Home debt, ditto, ditto	85,850,009	686,800
3	Pilgrimage to Mecca, and expenses connected with the Sacred Places	48,031,553	384,252 .
4	Civil List	156,734,871	1,253,878
5	Superannuations and charities	26,913,008	215,304
6	Grand Council and Tanzimat	14,920,646	119,365
7	Ministry of War	425,152,500	3,401,220
8	,, ,, Artillery	18,191,270	145,530
9	,, ,, Marine	98,850,205	790,801
10	,, ,, Tribunals	10,655,500	85,244
11	,, ,, Evcaff	19,042,666	152,341
12	,, ,, Interior	190,541,749	1,524,333
13	,, ,, Foreign Affairs	25,676,586	205,412
14	,, ,, Commerce and Public Works	9,742,504	77,940
15	,, ,, Public Instruction	2,802,478	22,419
16	,, ,, Police	13,796,664	110,373
17	,, ,, Finance	127,793,579	1,022,348
		1,386,073,678	11,088,583
18	Loss incurred on the retiring of metallic currency, charged upon 1276	32,667,000	261,336

1 and 2. *Interest of Debt.*

The foreign and home debts being, as regards the chief portion of them, subject to diminution by means of sinking funds, the charge for interest which in 1859-60 was about 1,578,000*l.* per annum, should decrease year by year, and such is actually the case as respects the foreign debt; but the exigencies of the Government are such that considerable sums of money have of late been raised in the capital at high rates of interest, so that the charge for the home debt has increased considerably, and is likely still further to increase.

A reduction in this charge is to be sought for in the measures adverted to in this Report for the regulation of the budget of receipts and expenditure, by which a surplus for the gradual redemption of the debt could be secured, and in those for the re-establishment of financial credit, by means of which money could be raised at a more moderate rate of interest than that which is now demanded for temporary loans obtained at the pressure of the moment.

3. *Pilgrimage to Mecca.*

The yearly pilgrimage which is sent to Mecca, and the expenses which are incurred at the Holy Places—Mecca, Medina, and Jerusalem—including repairs of mosques, khans, fountains, &c., and the salaries of officials, cost the large sum of 48,000,000 piastres, or about 380,000*l.*

Considering that the financial administration of Turkey has been found to be so lax at head-quarters, it is easy to believe that this large expenditure in a remote province of the Empire must be subject to great abuses. Such we are told is the case, and there is no doubt that by a rigorous investigation into the manner in which the money has been spent, followed by a reorganization of the administration of the funds, a large saving in the outlay could be made, and the balance could be applied more efficaciously than at

4. Civil List.

The Civil List of the Sultan, amounting to somewhat more than 1,200,000*l.* (which sum, however, large as it is, does not include the whole of the allowance for the Imperial establishment), is an item of expenditure with which there is considerable difficulty in dealing; for whatever sum is put down in the Budget, it rests entirely upon the will of the Sultan to restrain his expenses within the limit prescribed, or, on the contrary, to incur liabilities far beyond the amount which has been assigned to the Civil List. It is well known, that during the last few years a considerable portion of the financial deficits have arisen from the large amount of palace debts which have been thrown upon the public Treasury; but great hopes are now entertained, not only that the amount stated in the Budget will not be exceeded, but that His Majesty will continue the reforms which are said to have been begun in the Imperial establishments, so as to admit of a considerable reduction of the more than liberal amount now charged in the Budget. The successful reform of the Turkish financial system will be conditional on an amount of moral courage, on the part of all those who are in public authority, sufficient at least to induce them to submit to the restrictions and effect the economies necessary for the purposes of such a reform, and we believe the Sultan is fully sensible that this condition is not likely to be fulfilled unless the example is set by the Head of the Government.

5. Superannuations and Charities.

Superannuations and charities cost the State about 215,000*l.* a-year. Having regard to the number of officials at the capital, and the large salaries of the Officers of State and of the Governors of Provinces, this may not be a disproportionate amount, but we have reason to suppose that the grant of pensions depends too much upon the amount of influence the recipient may possess, and that a large portion is monopolized by the wealthy and powerful. We believe that it would be more in accordance with justice and with the good of the public service, if a regulated scale of pensions were introduced, to which deserving servants of the Government could look with confidence as a means of support when, after a life devoted to the public service, age or infirmity compels them to retire.

If the larger salaries were to be reduced, the burden of large pensions upon this fund should be diminished in the same proportion.

6. Grand Council and Tanzimat.

The charge for the Grand Council and Tanzimat in the year 1275 was about 120,000*l.* a-year, but in the year 1276 the salary of the President of the Tanzimat was reduced from 8,000*l.* to 6,800*l*, and that of the President of the Grand Council from 7,000*l.* to 5,800*l.*, and now by the consolidation of the two Departments some further saving will be effected in the salaries.

This Council bears some resemblance to the Privy Council in England, and acts as a Court of Reference and Appeal, but its utility is disputed by many, and we believe that at all events a still larger reduction might be made in the number of its highly-paid members without detriment to its efficiency.

7 and 8. Ministry of War and Artillery.

The charge for the War and Artillery Departments, including the Army, and all other military expenses, amounted for the year 1275 to somewhat more than 3,500,000*l.*, whilst the estimate for 1276 exceeds 4,000,000*l.*

In examining the detail of the Budgets, one cannot but be struck with the large cost of direction and superintendence, and with the high rate of remuneration which is paid to the higher classes of officials.

In England the cost of central direction and superintendence of the Military Departments is about 200,000*l.* a-year upon an expenditure of 14,600,000*l.*, or about $\frac{1}{73}$rd part of the total expenditure for military purposes; whereas, we find that in Turkey the cost is about 166,800*l.* upon an expenditure of 4,000,000*l.*, which places the proportion as high as $\frac{1}{24}$th part. This disproportion is easily accounted for when we observe that the Seraskier (Minister of War) receives a salary of about 16,000*l.* per annum; the Director-General of Artillery about 5,600*l.*; Conseiller-Général about 3,600*l.*; Conseiller of Artillery about 3,000*l.*; Paymaster-General about 3,500*l.*; Members of Supreme Council of War about 26,000*l.*; Members of Army Supplies about 5,700*l.*; Directors of Correspondence about 1,400*l.*; and others in a similar proportion.

On the other hand, we find that the clerks and subordinates are treated in a manner exactly the opposite. The bulk of these (531 out of 584) receive salaries at rates ranging, at the present course of exchange in the capital, from 10s. to 5l. per month, or 6l. to 60l. per annum.

Where the scale of remuneration is so extremely low, it may be supposed that many of the clerks, in the irregular attendance which they may choose to give, do not come to work but to learn business and to have the opportunity of pressing their claims for more lucrative posts, or merely to avoid being sent into the provinces; and it is to be feared that in some instances the opportunity of gaining extra official remuneration is not without its attractions. There is no scale of salaries, under which the clerks may look forward to an improved position according to their services, and it is only through interest that a higher rate of pay is obtained, so that the chief inducements for the display of zeal and intelligence are wanting.

The consequence is, that a staff of clerks is employed much larger than necessary, and amongst whom many are of little or no use as regards the work to be done, and the business of the Department is inefficiently performed.

We strongly recommend that not only in this office but in all the Departments of the Government there should be a complete reorganization of the numbers and salaries of the officials; that regularity of attendance during a fixed portion of the day should be insisted upon; that a larger number of clerks should not be employed than a fair distribution of work requires; that the exorbitant salaries of the higher officials should be reduced; that the body of the working clerks should receive remuneration adequate to the work they should be required to perform; and that the establishment of clerks should be divided into classes with annual rises and systematic promotion according to fixed rules.

The system of supplying the Civil Servants of the Crown with rations is also one which has lately been very properly discontinued. It is an expensive mode of supplying officials with what they either do not want, or with what they could purchase with greater advantage for themselves. The lower classes of officials are to receive an equivalent in money, and we believe that the cost of the articles converted into salary will not only be more acceptable to the clerks, but the Government will also be saved the expense and trouble of procuring and distributing the rations.

When we look to the army, for the management of which this Department is constituted, we find to a considerable extent the same defects.

The Commanders-in-chief of the several corps d'armée receive each of them in pay and rations 7,000l. or 8,000l. a-year, while the Conseil of each corps receive from 5,000l. to 7,000l. a-year, salaries far beyond what the finances of Turkey are able to bear.

The soldiers, on the other hand, receive but small pay, and are badly clothed and fed. By a readjustment of these charges greater efficiency would be obtained and even a saving upon the total expenses might be effected. The payment of the troops is conducted under the superintendence of the Colonel by a commission composed of all the commissioned officers of each regiment. Every evening the muster-roll is called, and the name of each man present is noted in a book kept for that purpose, and of which a copy is sent monthly to the War Department, bearing the seal of all the commissioned officers. The rations are charged according to the number of men shown in this book, and they are purchased by the commission of officers, the prices of each article being certified by the Kaimakam of the district and his Council in a formal declaration forwarded monthly to the War Department. The amount of pay drawn is based on the muster-roll or book referred to above. Another account of the number of men in hospital is sent up monthly certified by the doctor, the apothecary, and the hospital chief.

The correctness of the accounts is taken for granted by the War Department as they bear the seals of so many officers; but responsibility divided between so many is often less efficacious against error or fraud than when responsibility is more specially fixed upon individuals, and as regards the Turkish army it is commonly asserted, with what degree of truth we are unable to say, that the number of men charged and paid for on the muster-book is considerably larger than the actual strength of the regiments would warrant. Where all the officers are concerned in the payment they are all interested in bringing forward the largest claim against the Government, and there remains no independent body to check their proceedings.

We believe that it would be much more conducive to the correctness of the accounts and to economy, if Paymasters, to take entire charge of all regimental payments, directly responsible to the War Department, were to be appointed and their accounts were examined at head-quarters. In this case certificates and vouchers in support of the Paymaster's accounts, signed by officers, who would then be without personal interest in the money transactions of the regiment, would be a much greater check and security than their seals affixed to an account in which they are themselves concerned.

9. *Ministry of Marine.*

The observations which have been made with regard to the War Department apply with equal force to the Ministry of Marine.

In Turkey the total naval expenditure does not exceed 800,000*l.*, out of which the Admiralty or Department of Control costs 40,000*l.*, or one-twentieth of the total expenditure ; whereas we find that in England the proportion is not more than one seventy-fourth. ·

The salary of the Capudan Pasha, which was in the Turkish year 1275 about 10,000*l.* a-year, not being considered sufficient, was in the following year increased to about 13,000*l.* a-year, besides other sources of emolument.

The lower ranks of the officers and the sailors, on the other hand, receive miserable pay. The pay of a captain is about 40*l.* a-year, of a lieutenant 30*l.*, of a sub-lieutenant 15*l.* a-year, the sailors receive less than 3*l.* a-year. Rations and clothing are, however, supplied in addition to the rates of pay given above, and upon these may be said to rest the chief dependence of the officers and men, for their pay is generally many months in arrear, whereas the rations are dealt out with regularity. As the officers are entitled to several rations according to their rank, they are enabled by these means also to support their families.

With so small an expenditure as 800,000*l.* for the navy of the Turkish empire, it could hardly be expected that its fleet could be in a very satisfactory condition ; but when the manner in which this sum is spent is considered, it becomes a matter of surprise that the state of the navy is not worse than it appears to be. Here, as well as in the other offices of the Government, a complete reorganization of the Naval Department and of the rates of remuneration is required, not only in justice to the individuals, but as the best means of raising the efficiency of the service.

10. *Tribunals.*

The charge of 85,000*l.* for tribunals comprises the cost of the Central Administration at the capital, and includes the salaries of the Sheik-ul-Islam and the Ulemas, but most of the Judges and other officers of the Law Courts in the provinces receive remuneration in the shape of fees payable by the litigants, and it is asserted that in some instances (at Acre for instance) the office of Judge has been farmed out to the highest bidder.

We cannot speak too strongly against a system under which the administrators of justice are paid, not by fixed salaries, but by means of fees varying in productiveness according to the amount of litigation which can be attracted to their Courts, and if these fail to satisfy the wants of these officers they are exposed to the temptations which are held out to them on every side to accept extra-official remuneration which cannot fail to bias their judgments.

Liberal salaries should be paid to the Judges at the capital and in the provinces, and they should hold their appointments during good behaviour, and not be removable at the mere pleasure of the Government.

The additional expense which this would throw upon the country might in some measure be met by a well-regulated system of fees, which should not be payable as now to the officials, but to the public chest, and these would be most safely collected by requiring that all the proceedings of the Court should be founded upon documents impressed with a stamp equal to the amount of the fee to be paid.

11. *Evcaff Department.*

The charge for the Evcaff Department (Department for property devoted to sacred and charitable purposes) is about 150,000*l.*, which with the special revenues which belong to it, amounting to about 110,000*l.*, shows a total expenditure of 260,000*l.* a-year. The purposes to which these funds are devoted are so numerous, and often so minute, including the building, repairs, and charge of mosques, schools, fountains, khans, &c., that it is only by a vigorous and honest administration of its affairs in the capital and in the provinces that a proper application of the money can be secured.

The revenues of the Department, consisting partly of fixed contributions payable by a certain class of property, have fallen with the value of money, and the State has to bear the deficiency ; but we believe that with a better supervision this charge might be reduced, and the objects of the fund better carried out than, according to report, is at present the case.

12. *Ministry of the Interior.*

The Ministry of the Interior expends about 1,500,000*l.* a-year, which includes, however, some charges which more properly belong to the Civil List, such as presents made by the Sultan 50,000*l.*, and decorations 36,000*l.*, and extraordinaries are put down at 100,000*l.* The Grand Vizier's salary, which was 13,500*l.*, is still 11,000*l.*, and the Governors of provinces receive salaries varying from 4,000*l.* to 7,000*l.* The charge for coals, wood, &c., is 8,000*l.* a-year, and other items seem equally high. We believe that very large reductions might be made in many of these charges without detriment to the service.

On the other hand, the provincial police should be reorganized and better paid, so as to take away the inducement to increase their emoluments by exactions, which in some districts are so much complained of that the inhabitants have been heard to assert that they prefer the bandits to the police. An improved system has, however, been introduced in some districts with the best effect.

13. *Ministry of Foreign Affairs.*

The expenditure of the Ministry of Foreign Affairs was, for the Turkish year 1275, about 205,000*l.*, while the estimate for 1276 is only 130,000*l.*, showing a reduction on this head alone of 75,000*l.* How far the accounts, when made up, will show that these savings are real, we are unable to say; but we look upon these large reductions in the Estimates of this Department as some evidence that the same measures of retrenchment could be dealt out to the other Departments.

14. *Ministry of Commerce and Public Works.*

The expenditure of the Ministry of Commerce and Public Works amounted in 1275 to 78,000*l.*, and in the estimate for the following year a reduction is made of 20,000*l.*, which, however, does not fall upon the higher salaries or expenses of management, but is thrown entirely upon the head of repairs of streets, roads, bridges, &c.

This service does not appear to us to be the one upon which a reduction of expenditure should be effected ; indeed, looking at the lamentable state of these public works, and the impediments which trade and commerce have to contend with, owing to the want of proper means of transit and communication, we consider that the expenditure under this head, in place of being diminished, should be largely increased.

15. *Ministry of Public Instruction.*

About 20,000*l.* a-year is spent out of the Government Chest upon public instruction ; the Minister receiving one-fifth of the total sum. There are, however, a vast number of schools throughout the Empire supported by the mosques and by vacoof endowments, though the instruction in these is not carried beyond the art of reading and writing the Turkish language.

16. *Ministry of Police.*

The Ministry of Police costs about 110,000*l.* a-year, and does not call for special observation.

17. *Ministry of Finance.*

The charge for the Ministry of Finance for the Turkish year 1275 is more than 1,000,000*l.*, and the estimate for 1276 about 850,000*l.*, but this sum includes many charges which have little connection with the Department itself, viz., 50,000*l.* for meat supplied to the Palace which should appear in the Civil List charges ; more than 100,000*l.* for rations supplied to the Army, Navy, and other Departments ; above 100,000*l.* for repairs of forts, Government buildings, &c. ; 40,000*l.* for the chief Custom-houses ; 70,000*l.* for the Post Office and relays of horses ; 40,000*l.* for works at the mouth of the Danube ; 60,000*l.* for Circassian emigrants ; 16,000*l.* for coals and wood ; and other charges of a similar nature.

With regard to the more special expenditure of the Department we have to observe that the same defects appear to exist in the Finance Ministry that are found in the other Departments. The officers of direction and superintendence are much more numerous and more highly paid than necessary, while the working clerks receive a very low rate of salary.

The Office seems to be split up into a large number of small divisions, which entail an unnecessary number of chiefs, and we believe that if the business were placed, as we about to suggest, under the charge of three principal officers, and the minor divisions were done away with, a large saving in salaries might be effected, while the clerks might be more amply remunerated, and the work better performed.

18. *Miscellaneous.*

The Budget of the year 1276 includes a sum of about 260,000*l.*, payable as an indemnity to the Union Financière for a breach of engagement with respect to the withdrawal of the caimé, which affords an instance of the folly of attempting to direct the course of exchange by means of mere artificial arrangements.

On a general review of the whole of the expenditure of Turkey, it appears to us that there is great room for reduction of charges which could be combined with increased efficiency, but that, on the other hand, there are several services, especially those relating to Public Works, Roads, &c., to Courts of Justice, and to the Country Police, upon which a larger outlay is urgently required so soon as the state of the finances will admit of it. In any estimate, therefore, of the future demands upon the public exchequer, it will be prudent to look to an increase rather than a diminution in the rate of expenditure.

FINANCIAL ADMINISTRATION.

As regards the central administration and general control of the finances of this country, important changes are imperatively required. So great, indeed, is the importance of those changes that, unless they are effected, all other measures for the improvement of its financial condition would, as it appears to us, be of little value.

There is in Turkey no Minister of Finance, except in a very restricted sense of the term. There is a functionary bearing that title, who is a Member of the Council of Ministers, and assists at their deliberations. But his duties are little more than executive. He is charged with the receipt and custody of such part of the public revenue as is sent to th ecentral Treasury ; exercises a general superintendence over the collection of the taxes, and executes the decisions of the Government in regard to the public debt and to fiscal subjects generally. But a Minister specially responsible for the financial condition of the State, and to whom, therefore, the preparation of budgets, the balance of income and expenditure, and generally all subjects relating to taxation, and to the cost of administering the Government, are matters of peculiar concern, has no existence in this country. The executive duties of fiscal administration are (as we have said) performed by the Finance Minister; the deliberative by the Council of Ministers. The Ministers in Council agree upon the sum to be allotted to each of them for the purposes of his Department * during the current year, and a credit extending to that amount is opened in favour of each Department by the Minister of Finance, and the money issued to it in monthly instalments as required. These amounts are expended under the sole control of the different Ministers, and no account of the expenditure is rendered beyond a concise annual abstract, which is transmitted to the Finance Minister. Moreover, the limitation of the expenditure of each Department to the sum agreed upon and allotted to it is no more than nominal; since each Minister has the power of issuing "serghis," or obligations, for which there is no fixed date of payment, or, in other words, of contracting debts, without, so far as we can learn, any restriction whatever, and of which, indeed, no regular account is given,—the accounts which are sent annually to the Finance Minister by each Department showing only the amount of actual money payments which have been made.

It is evident that, so long as this system is maintained, a well-founded confidence in the state of the national finances is an impossibility. Where no one is specially responsible for the condition of the public purse, that condition is not likely to be very satisfactory. Where any member of the Government has power, by incurring liabilities without limit, to increase the debts of the State, there can be no security at any time for its solvency.

A reform in regard to this branch of the Administration is, in our opinion, urgently needed ; and the following are the principal measures and regulations which, as it appears to us, such a reform should comprise :—

The functions of the Minister of Finance should be defined by a spec al Imperial Edict.

The Minister of Finance should be responsible for the financial condition of the empire. He should propose, from time to time, the fiscal measures which he thinks necessary,

* Two Departments of the Government, viz., the Arsenal and the "Tidjaret," are endowed with special revenues, out of which a part of their expenditure is defrayed.

including those which relate to the public debt. He should receive from each Department, towards the close of each financial year, an estimate of the amount which will be required for the next. He should prepare the Annual Budget of the Empire. He should communicate the financial measures which he proposes, as well as the Budget which he has prepared, and the Departmental Estimates upon which it is based, to the "Conseil du Trésor," which should examine and report upon them. He should then lay them, with the Report of the "Conseil du Trésor," before the Council of Ministers, who should submit them, when approved, to the Sultan.

Immediately under the Minister of Finance there should be placed three officers: a Receiver-General, a Paymaster-General, and an Accountant-General.* The Receiver-General should, under the Minister, be responsible for the measures adopted for the collection of the revenue, and for its regular transmission to the Central or Provincial Treasury.

All the public revenues, of whatever kind (including those now specially assigned and paid to certain Departments of the Government), should in future be paid directly to the Receiver-General, or to his representatives in the provinces. The Receiver-General should render to the Finance Minister a daily account of his receipts during the day.

The Paymaster-General should be the only person authorized to disburse public money.

No payment, of whatever kind, should be made by any Department of the Government except by an order on the Paymaster-General.

All payments in the provinces on the part of the Government should be made by an order of the Paymaster-General on the Provincial chest.

Before the commencement of every month, each Department of the Government should submit to the Minister of Finance a statement of the amount which will be required during that month; and the Minister of Finance, after examining the statement, should authorize the Paymaster-General to meet the demands of the Department up to such an amount as he deems sufficient.

No Department should be allowed to exceed the sum which has been allotted to it in the Budget of the current year, with the following exceptions:—

Any Department which, from unforeseen circumstances, should find itself under the necessity of exceeding the sum so allotted to it, may make an application for the purpose to the Minister of Finance, who, after taking the opinion of the "Conseil du Trésor" upon the application, should lay it before the Council of Ministers, who, on approval, should submit it to the Sultan.

No orders for payment drawn by any Departments upon the Paymaster-General should be payable at a longer date than thirty days from the date of issue.

Each Department should send daily, or at short intervals, to the Paymaster-General a precise and detailed statement of the orders which it has given upon him.

The Paymaster-General should send to the Minister of Finance a daily Return of the payments which he has made during the day.

The Accountant-General should have charge of the general and detailed accounts of the Department, with the materials for which he should be supplied daily by the Receiver-General and the Paymaster-General.

He should keep the accounts relating to the debt, and assist the Finance Minister in the preparation of the Budget.

The accounts of the Finance Minister, as prepared by the Accountant-General, as well as those of each Department of the Government, should be submitted to a Board of Audit (Cour des Comptes), which should be constituted for the purpose, and which, after examining each account should append a report to it, and should submit the accounts and reports to the Council of Ministers.

No Government bond or obligation of whatever kind should be issued, except by the Minister of Finance.

Every proposal for an increase of the public debt, whether floating or permanent, internal or foreign, should be submitted by the Finance Minister for the approval of the Council of Ministers, after having taken the opinion of the "Conseil du Trésor" with regard to it.

In case it should be found necessary to issue Treasury obligations to meet the expenditure of the current year, in anticipation of in-coming revenue, the Minister of Finance should prepare a precise statement of the obligations which he proposes to issue, and of

---

* Under the present system Departments exist in the Ministry of Finance for receipts and payments respectively; but the duties of Receiver-General and Paymaster-General, as commonly understood, are for the most part discharged by the Minister of Finance himself.

the causes which render them necessary, and should submit such statement for the approval of the Council of Ministers.

The liquidation of these obligations should be secured as a first charge upon the public revenue, and they should be paid off, with the interest upon them, at a date not exceeding one year from the day of their issue, but at a shorter date if possible.

The annual Budget, together with such part of the Report of the " Conseil du Trésor " as may be necessary to justify or explain it, should be published, as soon as possible after it has been finally decided upon, in one or more of the principal Turkish and one or more of the principal foreign metropolitan journals.

The audited accounts of the several Departments, with the auditors' reports upon them, should also be printed and sold to the public at a moderate price.

These arrangements, thoroughly effected and rigorously maintained, would probably be sufficient to prevent any future disorganisation of the finances arising from the absence of individual responsibility, central control, and systematic regulation. The publication of the annual Budgets and accounts would supply the place, however imperfectly, yet so far as the nature of the case seems to admit, of the check which is imposed by popular institutions on financial mal-administration ; while the Minister of Finance would be guided and assisted in all questions of difficulty by a consultative body, and his proceedings subject to the general supervision and veto, if necessary, of the Ministerial Council.

It would be necessary, however, that the " Conseil du Trésor," which is to advise the Minister of Finance, should cease to be what it may almost be said to be at present, a merely nominal institution. This Council was brought together in November 1859, but reconstituted in its present shape in June 1860 (when the difficulties of the Government had become alarmingly serious) with considerable solemnity, and with the understanding, expressed publicly to the nation and to foreign Powers, that it was to take an active and most important part in the administration of affairs, as a deliberative body specially charged with the reform of the fiscal system, and with the future control and regulation of the finances of the empire. It consisted of six Ottoman subjects (of whom four were Turks) and three European members, viz., one recommended by the French Government, one by the British, and one by the Austrian Government ; the Secretary being also a European, recommended by the French Government. The Council has from that time to this been without any official definition of its functions. Its advice is but little resorted to, and when sought seldom acted upon ; and though it has rendered important service in reference to the preparation of regular Budgets, as well as in other respects, no opportunity has yet been given to it of preparing any general scheme of reform. At the present moment the resignation or removal of its members seems to threaten it with extinction. It now consists, we believe, of only five members, three of whom are Ottoman subjects and two Europeans ; nor can it be expected that those who remain will be long content to occupy a position which, if the present state of things continues, will be neither useful to the public nor creditable to themselves. It will be essential to the success of the measures which we have suggested that this Council should be re-constructed, and that its reality and efficiency should be assured. A further infusion of the European element would, as experience has shown, be highly conducive to its successful action. The number of Europeans should, we think, be fully equal to that of the Ottoman and Rayah members of the Council taken together, so that the former may not be out-voted by the latter. Thus reorganized and honestly upheld in its proper functions by the Government, there is no doubt that the Council would command the services of able and experienced men, and might perform the part assigned to it with the utmost advantage to the State.

ACCOUNTS.

The next point that calls for attention is the mode of accounting for the public revenue and expenditure.

That the accounts of a large Empire should be kept upon a proper system is a matter of the utmost importance ; for, without this, regularity and correctness in the pecuniary transactions of the country cannot be maintained, there can be no security that the whole of the revenue reaches the Government chest, nor that the payments which are charged have been properly expended ; and by the neglect of proper records, one of the best means of detecting fraud or embezzlement is lost.

Amongst other important advantages afforded by a clear and comprehensive system of accounts, is the facility it offers for acquiring a knowledge of the general condition of the country, and the assistance it gives in the study of questions connected with the sources of revenue, in regulating and controlling the receipts, in comparing the cost of the various heads of expenditure with the results produced by such expenditure, and generally in encouraging and facilitating financial inquiries.

.The opportunity that has been afforded us of inspecting the mode of conducting business in the public offices at Constantinople has led us to the conclusion that in the Ottoman Empire public accounts, as the term is ordinarily understood, can, except in one or two instances, scarcely be said to exist, and that consequently the knowledge upon financial matters is extremely limited.

Under these circumstances it is not to be wondered at that in a time of difficulty the finances of the country get into confusion, and that there should be a wide difference of opinion as to the remedies that should be applied.

There are, it must be admitted, many separate accounts and statements which are kept with the greatest neatness, and no doubt with accuracy, but no means are taken for classifying the items or bringing the results into one general view.

Accounts of the Finance Ministry.

The most important Department as regards accounts is that of the Minister of Finance. We have already pointed out what we consider to be the main defects in the constitution of this office, and have suggested that under the Finance Minister there should be three separate branches, having charge respectively of the receipts, the payments, and the accounts, with a responsible officer at the head of each who would relieve the Finance Minister of all the detail work of the Department with which his time is now taken up, and enable him to devote his attention to important measures of finance.

In order to explain more clearly the changes we would propose in the detail of the business, it will be well to describe the system which is at present pursued.

After the taxes and duties have been assessed in the manner shown in that portion of our Report which deals with the several sources of revenue, they are collected by officers subject to but little control, and the proceeds in the capital are paid into the Central Treasury chest, and those received in the Provinces are paid into the Provincial chests, which exist at the seat of government of each Province, under the charge of a Treasurer, controlled by the Governor and a Council.

The money received in the Provinces is to a considerable extent expended on the spot for provincial or other purposes, under directions of the Finance Minister, and the balance is remitted from time to time to the Treasury in Constantinople, the instructions directing that not more than 10,000 piastres shall remain in the hands of the Local Treasurer.

When payments are made out of the Provincial chests, the vouchers for such payments are transmitted to the Treasury as so much cash, which is brought to account as revenue, and the Department for which the payment was made is charged with the amount as an issue. A large portion of the revenue received in the Provinces is thus dealt with.

A monthly account of receipts and disbursements is sent from each Province to the Finance Minister, signed by the Treasurer, and certified by the Governor and the Members of the Council.

No vouchers accompany this account, and the examination it undergoes does not extend beyond comparing the balance brought forward with that shown on the previous account, and seeing that the remittances charged have duly reached the Treasury.

According to information which has been furnished to us from several quarters, and upon which we think considerable reliance may be placed, we are led to believe that with regard to these provincial accounts serious abuses exist.

We are told that in many cases the taxpayer is in ignorance as to the amount he is legally bound to pay; that, as it is not the practice to give written discharges for the sums paid, the payers are liable to be, and frequently are, called upon to pay the same amount of tax twice, and even three times over; that the members of the Council who certify the monthly accounts have little opportunity of knowing whether they are correct or not, but sign because it is the rule to do so, and because the Governor has done so; and that it is not unusual for the Treasurer to lend out at interest, for his own advantage, a portion of the balances in his hands, accounting for the deficiency by entering it in the account as arrears of taxes which have not been recovered.

How far these allegations are correct it would be difficult to say, but it seems evident that there is not sufficient check upon the Governor and Treasurer to prevent the existence of these abuses, and that in cases of fraud the chance of detection is very remote.

In order to diminish these opportunities for fraud, we would suggest the following modifications of the present system.

A list, containing a detailed statement, showing the taxes payable by each individual, should be prepared in each village, town, or district, and certified copies should be exposed in the most public places, such as at the entrance of mosques, churches, markets, &c., so that each taxpayer may know what he has to pay, and be able to see that he has not been overcharged in comparison with the other members of the community. A copy should also be transmitted to the Governor of the Province, and a second direct to the Finance Minister.

The collector should have a book of numbered receipts and counterfoils, upon each of which should be entered the particulars of the amount of tax payable, and for each sum paid he should deliver a corresponding receipt.

When the several communities remit the taxes received to the Provincial chests, the remittance should be accompanied by two lists, one showing the particulars of the sums received, the other those of the claims still outstanding.

The Governor should see that the sums returned as received are marked off in the list of taxes payable, which had previously been sent to him, and those which remain open should be compared with the list of claims outstanding.

The counterfoils of the receipts which have been delivered should also accompany the remittance, and be compared with the list of receipts.

Care should be taken that the list of taxes payable should be prepared and published by an authority distinct from and independent of the officer who has charge of the collection of them.

With these precautions, any questions which may arise between the taxpayers and the collectors, or between the latter and the Government, may readily be investigated and controlled.

When the remittance has been received at the Provincial Treasury, and the lists and counterfoils examined and marked off, the amount should be debited in a cash-book, arranged in columns for each class of tax, and on the creditor side should be entered the remittances to the Treasury and the local disbursements, supported by proper vouchers. The sums paid on account or in full should not be merely marked off on the back of the order, as is done at present, without any written acknowledgment of the money from the claimant, but separate receipts should in each case be given by the recipient.

After the end of each month a copy of the cash-book for that period, showing the balance at the commencement, the receipts and payments during the month, and the balance at the close of it, should be transmitted to the Finance Minister, signed by the Treasurer, and supported by the sub-accounts of the several communities, and by certificates from the Governor and certain members of the Provincial Council, declaring that the accounts have been duly examined and found correct. The signature of the accounts by the whole of the Council appears to divide the responsibility too much, and it would seem desirable that two or three of the Council should be selected as auditors, and be held responsible for the correctness of the accounts.

When the Provincial accounts have reached the Treasury at Constantinople, they should be carefully examined and compared with the sub-accounts; and although it may not be necessary in all instances to subject the sub-accounts to a detailed examination, it will be useful to do so occasionally, especially where there is reason to doubt their correctness.

We would also propose that a staff of Finance Inspectors should be maintained under the direction of the Finance Minister, who should constantly be employed in the Provinces, inspecting and reporting upon the accounts of the Treasurers, and the mode of assessing and collecting the taxes in the country. They should, as far as possible, investigate matters in dispute and complaints, which, in minor matters, they should have the power of deciding upon themselves, while more important questions should be referred by them, with a report, to the Finance Minister for his decision.

We need scarcely observe how necessary it would be that the officers selected for this important duty should be men of intelligence and of undoubted probity and integrity; and it would also be desirable that the inspectors should be frequently moved from one Province to another, in order to avoid their becoming mixed up with local or personal interests.

At the Ministry of Finance ("Malié"), three books of accounts are kept for the record of the general business, viz., a book of receipts, a book of payments, and a memorandum book to show the daily balance in hand.

In the receipt book are entered consecutively each day, first, such sums as are received directly at the Treasury, and then the gross amount of receipts debited in the Provincial accounts, as they arrive at the capital and are examined. The total amount of the receipts is entered in one sum, and there is no classification of the sources of revenue from which they have been derived.

When sums have to be paid to the Treasury the payer obtains a certificate of the amount from the office of Registry, which he hands to the Cashier with the money. The latter certifies the payment of the sum to the chest, upon which the Finance Minister himself signs a definitive receipt, should it even be for the smallest sum.

The payments are dealt with in the same manner, the entries in the book showing the imprests to other Departments on account of their yearly grants, the payments made at the Treasury for other purposes, and, in one sum, the total amount of payments charged in the Provincial accounts.

In the memorandum-book the total amount of each day's receipts is added to the balance remaining from the previous day, and the amount of payments is deducted, showing the balance in the chest at the close of the day. The Finance Minister receives a statement of the balance each morning, and, at intervals, himself counts the money to see that it agrees with the sum appearing in the memorandum-book.

The monthly Provincial accounts, after they have been recorded, are put away in bags, each Province (of which there above 100), having its own special bag. These bags are stowed away in boxes, which are locked up in a strong-room.

The deficiencies of such a system are evident.

In order to ascertain the produce of any tax or other source of revenue, it is necessary to search through the ·book of receipts and through each of the monthly Provincial accounts, amounting to more than 1,000, and extract from them each item applicable to the source of revenue in question. This is rendered still more difficult by the system of farming out certain of the taxes, for in some cases the smaller taxes of a town or district are sold in a mass, the Finance Minister himself having but a very vague idea of what these taxes consist, as they vary in different districts.

By this entire want of classification the Finance Minister is deprived of the important advantage of watching from time to time the progress of each source of revenue, and of comparing against previous years the produce of each tax, either generally or in any individual Province. By the absence also of the entry of details, the Provincial accounts escape an excellent check upon their correctness.

The same remarks apply to the records of the payments, though in a smaller degree, as these transactions are confined at the Treasury to the payment of some of the official salaries and minor expenses, and to the issue of periodical sums to the principal Departments of Government who conduct their own payments.

The mode also of checking the balance by daily addition and deduction in place of carrying the receipts to one side of a cash book, and the payments to the other, does not even afford the means of seeing from time to time what have been the total amounts of the receipts and payments during the portion of the year that may have elapsed.

That the other accounts of the Treasury are not in a more satisfactory condition may be judged from the fact that the preparation of a very incomplete statement of the debts and liabilities of the Empire has required a period of more than three months.

It has already been stated that in making payments, the order presented by the claimant is retained by the cashier, but no written acknowledgment is given by the recipient for the money.

In the case of merchants, bankers, contractors, and others, where the claims are large and sums are paid on account, a statement of the claim is prepared in duplicate, of which the Finance Minister retains one copy, and the claimant holds the other. When a sum is paid on account it is written off from the amount appearing due on each copy, but here again no receipt is given for the sum paid.

It is evident that this system offers great facilities for fraud and collusion, especially when it is remembered that official documents are written with Indian ink on highly glazed paper, and in case an alteration in the writing is required, an application of the tongue is much more effectual than an eraser.

The absence of vouchers for each payment is also a great impediment to the due record of the transactions of the Department.

Another difficulty in regard to the accounts arises from the different kinds of money in which the pecuniary operations of the country are·carried on.

In the Provinces cash transactions are principally conducted in a debased silver coin called " beshliks," while in the capital they are in " caimé," an inconvertible paper money which now passes current at a very large discount.

In the accounts of the Finance Ministry these two classes of money are not kept distinct, but paper piastres, worth now about 240, and metallic piastres worth about 120 to the 1*l.* sterling, are entered in the same column. It is averred that the chief portion of the revenue received in metallic is also paid away in the provinces before reaching the capital, but still a considerable portion does reach the chest of the Treasurer at the Malié, and if he feels inclined to substitute 120 paper piastres for the same number of metallic, he takes out of the chest the value of 1*l.*, and puts back what is worth only 10*s.*, without in any way affecting the accounts.

The Finance Minister informed us that a daily memorandum was furnished to him showing the proportion of paper and metallic of which the balance consists, but as this statement cannot be checked by the accounts it can be but of little value.

We propose in order to remedy these defects that a complete system of account-books should be introduced at the Finance Ministry. Detail books should be established in which each receipt or payment should be entered under its proper head, and should be abstracted daily and carried into a cash book kept in the debtor and creditor form; the monthly totals should be passed through a journal into a ledger upon the double entry system, so that not only the details of the pecuniary transactions of the Government may be duly recorded, but that the general results and the financial position of the country may be seen at a glance during any month of the year.

Each of these books should be supplied with double money columns in order to keep separate the metallic from the paper-money, so that a daily control may be kept upon the amount of each which should be found in the chest.

The knowledge of accounts in Turkey is, however, so extremely limited that it would be almost hopeless to attempt to introduce these ameliorations without special assistance being procured for the purpose from some country where there already exists a knowledge of the science of book-keeping, with practical experience in its adaptation to public accounts.

Two or three experienced officers, well versed in Government accounts, aided by a few intelligent accountants, who might easily be found on the spot, would have little difficulty in bringing the accounts into order, provided the necessary facilities and encouragement were given to them by the Turkish Government.

Accounts of the Ministry of War and Admiralty.

The accounts kept at the Seraskeriat (Ministry of War) and the Arsenal (Admiralty) are still more defective.

In those Departments there exists a special Council for the purpose of examining and passing demands under contracts and other claims. When payment is demanded, the Secretary and the Treasurer, after satisfying themselves that the claim has been duly passed by the Council, issue an order for its payment in duplicate, either for the full sum or for a sum on account. One of the duplicates is sent to the cashier, the other is handed to the claimant, and when the latter presents the document for payment, the cashier compares it with his own duplicate, and if it agrees he pays the amount ordered, writing off the sum paid on the back of each document. The receipts and payments are entered in the same book. First come the receipts of the day, and then upon the same page follow the payments. The daily totals are carried into a memorandum-book, in which the receipts are added each day to the previous balance, and the payments are deducted, showing the balance at the close of the day.

This appears to be the whole of the system of accounts at these offices. If it is wished to ascertain the amount of expenditure upon any head of service, the different items have to be picked out of the daily account and added together. There are no abstract books, no ledger, no books in which the accounts of merchants and contractors are entered. These latter are kept on slips of paper which show at the beginning the sum due, and then each instalment on account is deducted as it is paid until no balance remains, the claimant not being called upon to give a receipt or any written acknowledgment for the sum that is paid him.

The balance in the hands of the cashier is occasionally checked by the memorandum-book; but neither the accounts nor the documents are examined after payment either by the Council or elsewhere.

It is evident that under this system there must exist great opportunities for fraud, and should the Treasurer and Secretary combine for this purpose there does not appear to be any check to bring to detection the fraudulent issue of an order for the payment of a sum not legally due.

The authorities granted by the Council should be duly recorded before payment, and the accounts and documents should, after payment, be sent to the Council, or to some officer appointed for the purpose, for examination, in order to see that the payments have not been in excess of the sums passed by the Council, and that they have been made to the proper parties.

It may be readily understood that the financial difficulties under which the country is at present suffering render it impossible for the Treasury to supply the several Departments with funds sufficient to meet at once the whole of the claims as they fall due. It is therefore the practice of these Departments (as we have observed in our remarks upon the general direction of the finances) to issue orders, called "serghis," for which, however, no special date of payment is fixed.

It is quite uncertain when these "serghis" will be liquidated, as this depends upon the means of meeting them, and upon the amount of pressure or influence the holders are able to bring to bear upon the officials of the Department by which the orders were issued. No notice is taken of these orders in the accounts of the Department until they have been actually paid.

It thus occurs that a large expenditure may be going on without there being any trace of it in the public accounts, and an order for payment which has been issued from the Admiralty at one date may not appear as expenditure till many months afterwards, rendering it impossible to obtain a just view of the liabilities and expenditure of the Department at any given time.

To obviate these inconveniences we would recommend that when there are not sufficient funds to meet the expenditure, the "serghis" or orders for payment should be at once entered in the books of accounts as expenditure, and the Departmental orders should be exchanged on presentation at the Finance Ministry for Treasury obligations, which should be numbered and dated, and be paid in the order in which they are issued, as soon as there are funds to meet them.

These obligations would then take the shape of floating debt chargeable to the Finance Ministry in place of outstanding claims on account of expenditure which has been incurred but has not been recorded.

While referring to this subject it will not be inopportune to give our opinion upon the subject of incurring liabilities upon credit without any limit as to the period of payment. It is evident that when the date of payment may be indefinitely postponed, and where the value of money varies with a rapidity unknown in other countries, the only safe mode for a contractor to enter into contracts for the supply of goods is to fix such a price as would be remunerative at the worst rate of exchange and at the most distant date of payment. The Government therefore pays for the supplies it requires a price infinitely higher than it would pay were the period of payment made short and fixed.

We believe, therefore, that the great saving in expenditure which might be effected by meeting all liabilities with promptness and regularity would be sufficient amply to compensate for the cost which would be incurred by the necessity of raising at a high rate of interest money for the purpose of carrying out this arrangement. A system of regularity in discharging liabilities would also put a stop to the mischievous practice which now exists among merchants and other claimants of paying large fees to the officials in order to obtain preference in the payment of their claims.

The stores belonging to the Admiralty are under the charge of a storekeeper, but as far as we could discover no accounts are kept to check the receipt or issue of stores.

The only book which was produced to us was a rough memorandum-book in which the transactions were entered as they occurred without order or regularity, the receipts and issues of goods being all mixed up together in such confusion that an attempt to check the stock of articles on hand would be hopeless.

Accounts of the Custom-house Department.

At the Custom-house we found a far superior system of accounts in operation, and the present Director is giving his attention to further improvements for which there is still room.

The accounts of this Department are now kept by double-entry under the superintendence of some intelligent Coptic accountants, who have been brought from Egypt for this purpose.

There are, however, still considerable defects which require remedy.

After the examination of goods landed for payment of duties at the Custom-house has taken place in the unsatisfactory manner already described in an earlier portion of our Report, one copy of the note of quantities is given to the merchant, and a second is delivered to the Accountant's Department. The First Clerk thereupon makes upon a loose sheet of paper the calculations of the duties payable according to the Tariff, a Junior Clerk checks it, and it is then submitted to the Chief Clerk. On his approval the results only are entered in a book, and the paper of calculations is destroyed. These papers should be preserved, or the full particulars should be entered in a book before they are checked; for under the present plan the destruction of the original document, which has been subjected to careful examination, prevents the discovery of any discrepancies owing to

F

error or fraud which may occur in making the entries of the mere results in the account-book, and it would be impossible to fix the responsibility of such errors upon any individual in particular.

A note of the amount payable upon each importation is sent to the merchant, and as there are no bonding warehouses it is usual to give three months' credit. Where the transactions are numerous a monthly demand is sent to the merchant, who compares it with the separate notes previously sent, and if he finds it to be correct, he gives in return a bill of exchange for the amount at three months' date, which if not met when due, being in the hands of Government, becomes a first lien on the estate of the merchant. We are told that losses of revenue by the defalcation of merchants are now of rare occurrence.

Formerly merchants were allowed to keep their accounts with Government for duties open for long periods, and large sums were lost by this system of long credit, but these monthly settlements by bills of exchange have remedied this evil.

The money as received at the Custom-house, as well as any payments on account of salaries and expenses, are entered in a cash-book, kept in the debtor and creditor form, and the money transactions of the Department are passed through a journal into a ledger kept upon the double-entry system, but still in a defective manner. In the journal the debits and credits are placed in the same column, and they are not totalled, so that it does not act as a check upon the ledger.

The ledger is also very imperfect, and does not contain more than a dozen accounts. All the merchants' accounts are combined in one general personal account, in place of each merchant with whom there are current transactions having a separate account. The duties received from all sources are entered under one head, so that it is impossible to tell the amount of duty which the several articles of import and export have produced. This renders it very difficult to arrive at any just estimate of the progress of the various branches of trade or industry of the country, but we believe that the present Director of the Constantinople Custom-house has the intention of introducing accounts to obviate this defect.

The salaries and expenses of the Custom-house are paid out of the revenue in hand, but they are correctly charged as expenditure, and the gross revenue is brought to account.

Until lately most of the Provincial Custom-houses have been farmed, and, amongst other disadvantages, one result has been that the Government has no accounts whatever at these ports, as all that it has looked to has been to obtain the highest amount of rent and to receive the instalments with regularity.

As now, however, the direction of the Custom-house in Roumelia and the collection of the duties have come under the direct charge of the Government, and as the farming system may shortly cease in the Asiatic Provinces also, it becomes of the highest importance that accounts upon the most approved system should be introduced at the head office at the capital and be extended to the other ports of the empire, and that the Provincial Custom-houses, in place of being under the control of the Finance Minister, as some are at present, should be entirely placed under the direction of the Director of Customs at Constantinople, who should be supplied with a staff of able and trustworthy accountants, for the purpose of framing and directing the accounts. In order to do this effectively it would be very desirable to get assistance from the west of Europe, from whence experienced officers could no doubt be obtained to guide and instruct the others.

Accounts of the Evcaff Department.

The accounts of the Evcaff, the Department having charge of a vast amount of property devoted to religious and charitable purposes, were formerly kept in a very inefficient manner, and it is stated that great abuses exist in the management of these funds.

The Minister, however, who was appointed to take charge of this Department since our arrival here had commenced the introduction of a superior system of accounts, and by his reforms had, in the few months of his administration, greatly improved the financial position of this Department. We heard, therefore, with regret that this intelligent officer had been dismissed.

Accounts of the Bureau d'Amortissement.

The accounts at the Bureau d'Amortissement, the office charged with the sinking funds of the "consolidés" and the "hasnè tahvilis," are also kept in a very satisfactory manner, and the persons who have carried out these improvements might well be employed on more important accounts.

As far as we can learn the accounts of other Departments are in no better condition than those of the War Department and Admiralty, and there seems but little chance of their being brought into proper order unless the Porte will consent to employ a sufficient staff of able accountants, and will support those who have the energy to carry out improvements.

We have already referred to one change which we wish strongly to recommend, and which applies to all the Departments of the Government. Under the present system each Department receives monthly sums from the Finance Minister, which it disburses through its own cashier. Each Department has its own pay-office, its own chest, and a special balance of money under its control.

We have already suggested that no payments in money beyond certain petty disbursements should be made in any public offices, except at the Treasury, but that the whole of the payments of the Administrative Departments should be made by orders upon the Paymaster-General, who would make the payments under the direction of the Finance Minister.

Each Department would charge the order for payment as expenditure. The accounts would be simplified and expedited, the balance of public money would be economized, and the accounts of the Treasury would act as a check upon those of the other Departments.

The receipts and payments of the Treasury, after they have been duly recorded by the Accountant-General, as well as the accounts of the several Departments, should be referred, as we have suggested in a former part of our Report, to a Board of Audit, which should be composed of officers thoroughly conversant with public accounts.

The staff of accountants to be employed in introducing an improved system of accounts should be placed under the direction of this Board, so as to secure uniformity of accounts throughout the whole of the public offices, and the several Departments should be bound to adopt the recommendations of the Board in the arrangement of their accounts.

BALANCE OF REVENUE AND EXPENDITURE.

The expenditure of the current year, 1861-62, is estimated to exceed the receipts by 212,223,375 piastres, or about 1,700,000*l*.* To this, however, must be added a sum which is given in the list of debts as a separate liability, but which ought to have been included in the deficit of this year, 152,346,500 piastres, or about 1,220,000*l*., representing the loss to the Government under different items of expenditure which have had to be met by payments in metallic, and which loss is consequent on the present high rate of exchange caused by the depreciation of paper money.

The total estimated deficit of the current year is therefore about 364,000,000 piastres, or about 2,920,000*l*.

Such being the present deficit, we have now to consider what will be the amount for which, as regards future years, either by reduction of expenditure or by increase of income, provision must be made.

Although the sum last mentioned (152,346,500 piastres), is properly to be treated as part of the current deficit, its existence is the result of a state of things to which there is an absolute and immediate necessity of putting an end. It represents, in fact, a part of the price paid by the Government for a loan of that most costly and ruinous kind which consists in the issue of inconvertible paper. Among the remedial measures which must be adopted to meet the present emergency is included the withdrawal of the paper money of the Government, which (if a loan cannot be obtained) must be effected gradually, by means of a certain amount of public revenue annually set apart for that purpose. If this is done under regulations such as to inspire public confidence, the result must be an immediate enhancement of the value of the paper money; and the sum in question (of 152,346,500 piastres) will be still further reduced by the agreement which (we understand) has been made by some, and is likely to be made by other States having Treaties with Turkey, to pay the Custom duties of Constantinople in

* The actual deficit for the year 1860-61 is stated in the list of debts at 150,277,065 piastres, or about 1,202,000*l*. The estimated deficit, therefore, for the year 1861-62 exceeds by 61,946,310 piastres, or about 498,000*l*., the actual deficit for the past year. We have been unable to obtain the details of this estimate, and therefore to ascertain in what manner this increase of deficit is to be accounted for; but, inasmuch as the receipts for the year 1861-62 are estimated at about the same sum as that to which they amounted in 1860-61, it is, of course, clear that the increase must arise from an addition to the expenditure. It is probable that this addition proceeds from extraordinary expenditure, as, for instance, from that incurred on account of the Montenegrin difficulty; but as we have no means of judging to what extent this is the case, we have thought it advisable to take the estimated deficit of 1861-62 (about 1,700,000*l*.) as the basis for an estimate of the probable requirements of the State for the next few years.

metallic money. If, in addition to this, the measures which we have suggested, or are about to suggest, for the re-adjustment of the balance sheet and the improvement of the financial administration, are adopted without delay, the effect will, in all probability, be to re-establish public credit, and as a consequence to raise the paper money of the Government to its full nominal value.

We think, therefore, that in estimating the amount which will be required for future years, this sum of 152,346,500 piastres may be excluded from consideration.

We have, then, in the first place, to provide for a probable excess of expenditure over income of 1,700,000*l.*

In the next place, it will be necessary to place a certain fixed charge upon the revenue, for the purpose of dealing with fiscal liabilities and difficulties which can no longer be postponed. There can be little doubt that an annual sum of 500,000*l.*, judiciously applied, would be sufficient for this object, whether it were used for the purpose of obtaining a loan (supposing that course possible), which would serve to withdraw the existing paper and to supersede the necessity of a further issue, or for the withdrawal by annual instalments of the whole amount of paper which is already in circulation, or which remains to be issued.

The annual sum, therefore, for which, on this estimate, it becomes necessary in future years to provide, either by diminution of expenditure, or by increase of receipts, is in all about 2,200,000*l.* (275,000,000 piastres).

In considering the means by which this sum may be obtained, we do not hesitate to say that a material reduction of the aggregate expenditure of the country is an expedient which we should recommend for adoption only in case it should be absolutely impossible to devise any other. As we have shown, important economies might easily be effected in several branches of the expenditure, as, for instance, with regard to the Civil list, and to the salaries of the higher class of employés, and a considerable diminution of expenditure may be expected to arise from the reforms which we have suggested in regard to the general administration of the finances, and to the mode of keeping the public accounts. But the whole of the revenue which might thus be saved is urgently required for the service of the country. It can scarcely be said that a revenue of 12,000,000*l.* is too large for the due administration of the affairs of an empire such as that of Turkey. It is true that a considerable portion of this revenue is misapplied and ill-administered; but simply to reduce it by that portion, while some of the most urgent necessities of the country remain unsatisfied, would be a measure economical only in appearance. With an army scarcely sufficient to ensure the defence of the frontier from marauding tribes, and power-less in the face of a fanatical outbreak; with a police which, in many parts of the Empire, casts not even the shadow of restraint upon the thriving trade of brigandage; with production and commerce paralyzed for want of roads; and a judicial system requiring great and expensive improvements,—it must be admitted that the mode of redressing a balance-sheet which consists in a mere reduction of expenditure would be costly in the extreme to this country. On the other hand, the resources of the Empire are admitted to be immense, and its taxation only burdensome in so far as it is ill-adjusted.

It is, therefore, we think to the revenue side of the account that recourse must be had for the means of placing the income of the Empire in the required relation to its expenditure.

There can be no question but that when the measures which have already been taken by the Government, as well as those (supposing them to be taken) which we have recom-mended, have produced their full effect, the increase in the receipts of the Treasury will be sufficient to provide not only the additional sum which we have found to be requisite, but one of far greater amount. The gain to the revenue which may be expected to arise from the relief given by the readjustment of the " verghi," from the direct collection of the " dîme," from the abolition of the export duties, from stamps, from tobacco, from the proper management of mines, fisheries, and other public property, and especially from the making of roads, will be sufficient to place it in, to say the least, a prosperous condition. The construction of roads, even if confined in the first instance to some of the more important agricultural districts, would in itself suffice to produce a great and permanent increase of national income. Amongst other evils caused by the want of roads is, that it reduces the price of produce in the interior to such an extent that while corn is selling at the seaboard at 30 or 40 piastres the kilo, the same quantity of produce will not produce to the cultivator in the interior more than 4 or 5 piastres, the cost of freight exceeding the difference of value. A threefold loss arises to the Government in conse-quence:—

1. The Government obtains only the small local value for the share of produce which falls into its hands in the shape of " dîmes " in place of the increased value which a ready

means of transport would give to what is the largest and most important source of the revenue of Turkey.

2. As export from the inland country becomes impossible, the cultivation of agricultural produce cannot be extended beyond the local wants of the district, and, consequently, the Government receives " dîmes " on a very limited production.

3. The indigence of the agricultural population, caused by this want of inducement to increase their produce, diminishes, to a great extent, their consumption of articles paying import duties, and the amount received from them on account of other taxes.

The new law respecting roads shows at least an intention on the part of the Government of dealing with this important subject. The principle of that measure, viz., that of entrusting the different communities with the task of constructing and repairing, at their own expense, the roads of their several districts, leaving to the Government little more than the cost of administration and professional superintendence, appears to us to be sound. And although without an intimate acquaintance with the internal condition of the country, it is impossible to form a judgment as to the probable success of the law, and especially as to the expediency of effecting the object in view by means of personal service, rather than of a highway rate, we should hope, now that the supreme importance of that object has been recognized by the Government, that every effort will be made to overcome any difficulties of execution, or, if necessary, to devise some more effectual scheme.

Among the impediments which exist to commercial prosperity, and therefore to a flourishing condition of the revenue in this country, must be noticed the system of " Esnaffs," or Corporations, under which, as regards many trades and pursuits, a monopoly exists, which, by excluding competition, prevents the advancement which the skill and energy of intelligent or industrious individuals would otherwise produce. And the first evil brings with it a second; for, in order to prevent the monopolists from charging unreasonable prices, the Government is again obliged to interfere, and dictate the prices at which the articles or produce are to be sold. Meat, bread, and even garden-produce, are subjected to these regulations; and in cases of failure of crops, it frequently occurs that the prices fixed do not remunerate the producers, and production ceases at a time when it should be especially stimulated. We strongly recommend the removal of these interferences with the free course of demand and supply.

For similar reasons, it is most desirable that an end should be put to the custom which obtains in some districts, amongst others in the Government of Salonica, of prohibiting the peasantry from leaving the estates of landholders without their sanction. We have even heard of cases where peasants have been ordered to return after an absence of ten years. This attempt artificially to regulate labour and production by Government control can only result in injury to the State and to the people.

But the operation of most of these measures, directly or indirectly conducing to the increase of the revenue, must necessarily be gradual, and (supposing that they are all adopted) they will effect comparatively little for the next few years to come. It becomes necessary, therefore, to consider by what new imposts or other fiscal measures the requisite annual amount (2,200,000*l.*) may be obtained.

Taxation of Constantinople.

Among these, that which is entitled to the first place because it is called for by considerations, not only of expediency, but of mere justice, is a measure which would compel the Capital to bear for the future its due share of taxation.

The exemption of Constantinople and its environs from direct taxes not only deprives the Treasury of a large sum which it might legitimately claim, but inflicts a great wrong upon the tax-paying community, and has the further disadvantage of producing an unnatural determination to the Capital of wealth and social position which are greatly needed for the improvement, moral and material, of other parts of the Empire. Whatever reasons may have existed for the original exemption, there can be none for its continuation at the present time; and we cannot believe that a mere traditionary custom will any longer be allowed to prevail against the yearly increasing claims of distributive justice and the urgent necessities of the national exchequer.

A step in the right direction has, we believe, been recently contemplated by the Government, and the draft of a law "sur la patente " prepared, by which a duty is to be imposed on all shops, warehouses, and other places of commercial business, at the rate of 8 per cent. on the rent of those which have not had a monopoly, and 4 per cent. on that of those which have had, but are no longer to have one, and of 12 per cent. on places in which banking is carried on; with a further annual impost, averaging from about ½ to

1½ per cent. on the rent, in the shape of a fee for a "teskereh" or permission to trade.* No estimate appears to have been made as to the yield of the proposed tax, and we are unable to conjecture, even approximately, its probable amount ; but from the few data which exist on this subject, we should suppose that it would not be more than from 50,000*l.* to 100,000*l.* per annum.

Such a measure, however, would obviously be but a small instalment of that which is really required, and which is to tax, in fair proportion, the accumulated wealth and luxury of the capital. The mode of effecting this object which most naturally suggests itself, is the application to Constantinople and its neighbourhood of the "verghi" or income tax, as paid in all other places throughout the Empire. There are, however, some objections to this course. The provinces are accustomed to the "verghi" itself, to the machinery by which it is assessed, and to the inequalities unavoidable, or otherwise, of its operation. The capital would not only have to bear an entirely new tax, but to submit to a process of inquisitorial assessment of which it has had no experience, and to an inequitable incidence which it would ill tolerate. We are disposed to think, therefore, that the new impost should not be the "verghi" itself, but a modification of it. There can be little doubt that the rent of a dwelling-house is, in general, no unfair test of the relative wealth of the person occupying it ; and we should propose that a certain fixed sum should be imposed upon Constantinople in the way of "verghi," which should be divided among the resident householders, the share which is paid by each individual being proportionate to the rent or annual value of the house which he occupies ; all houses below a certain rental, and also (in the event of the execution of the new projected law "sur la patente") all shops, warehouses, and other places of business subject to the new law, being exempted from the tax.

It remains to consider what should be the amount of the proposed contribution. The materials for forming an accurate judgment upon this question are altogether wanting, though there can be little doubt that a sum amounting to several hundred thousand pounds sterling per annum might safely be imposed. In the year 1859 a tax which was laid for one year upon the owners of houses in Constantinople and its environs, but which was only partially levied, of 10 per cent. on the rental in cases where the house was let, and 5 per cent. in cases where it was occupied by the owner, and a further impost on persons engaged in trade of 10 per cent. on the rental of their place of business, was estimated by the Government to yield 35,000,000 piastres. If we suppose the last-mentioned tax (on the rental of places of business) to have been taken as yielding one-third of the whole amount, there would remain a sum of about 23,000,000 piastres as the estimated result of the tax on dwelling-houses. Assuming this sum to represent on the average 8 per cent. on the rental, and the rental to be one-fifth of the income of the occupier, it will be found that an impost of 70,000,000 piastres, or 560,000*l.*, would be equivalent to a tax of somewhat less than 5 per cent. on the aggregate income of occupiers of dwelling-houses. This sum, therefore, might (as it would appear) fairly be fixed as an annual payment upon the capital. Some deduction must, however, be made from it on account of the exemption which we have suggested of houses below a certain rental to be afterwards determined, and also for any loss which may be occasioned by the refusal of foreigners to pay the tax ; but allowance being made on these accounts, a sum of fully 500,000*l.* might (it would appear) safely be taken as that which (according to the estimate of the Government on the occasion referred to) Constantinople and its neigh-bourhood should be required to pay.

Foreign residents in Turkey, who under the "Capitulations" (as they are termed) of their respective Governments, claim (with what justice it is not within our province to inquire) exemption from all taxation which can in any sense be considered personal, will, we presume, pay this tax, if they pay it at all, only in the way of a voluntary contribution. We would venture to suggest that the time has arrived when those States which desire the prosperity of Turkey should endeavour to effect some equitable arrangement with respect to this anomalous exemption, which originated in a state of things very different to the present, and which is the cause of no inconsiderable loss and embarrassment to the Turkish Government. It can hardly be expected, however, that any privileges which foreigners may be held to possess in this respect should be abandoned so long as they are excluded from proprietary rights in Turkey ; nor, on the other hand, could the Porte be fairly required to grant such rights to foreigners, so long as the houses which they occupy are exempt from liability to the visits of the police, and may thus afford shelter to criminals and impunity to crime. The natural basis, therefore, of any such arrange-

* As regards this fee, the difficulty arising from the claims of foreigners to exemption is met by requiring that each lease shall contain a provision in which the owner of the place of business for which the lease is granted guarantees the payment of the fee.

ment would be, on the one hand, the concession to foreigners of the right to hold property in their own names, and, on the other, the assimilation of their position to that of Ottoman subjects in regard both to the payment of taxes and to the authority of the police. On the part of those foreign nations which are in the habit of treating Turkey as a civilized and friendly State, such a modification of existing Treaties would have both justice and consistency to recommend it; while the Porte, which is (as we have had already occasion to notice) seriously injured in its fiscal interests by the restriction in regard to the tenure of property, would, probably, gain more by that which it conceded than by that which it received in return.

Domestic Servants.

A tax on male servants would, in Turkey, be characterized by almost every element of fiscal expediency. The inordinate number of male servants employed in this country, and the amount of waste, idleness, and useless display which are its consequences, are obvious and notorious; and a tax which would yield a large sum to the Treasury, and, while falling wholly on the superfluities of life, and tending to the restraint of luxurious habits, would, at the same time, set free for productive employment capacity for labour which is now lost to the community, is one which needs but little argument to recommend its adoption.

The statistics necessary for a conjecture as to the sum which might be obtained from such an impost are wanting, and any estimate which we could form of it must be somewhat vague. So far, however, as we are able to judge from inquiries which we have made on the subject, we should suppose that the number of male servants in Turkey might be safely stated as at least 500,000, on which number a tax of 1*l.* per head would produce a gross sum of 500,000*l.* This sum would probably be but little diminished by the cost of collection, which would be effected in the provinces by existing machinery; but it may be well to allow a margin on this account, and to place the annual amount which might be anticipated from this source at 450,000*l.* (56,250,000 piastres). The tax should include all caïquejis (boatmen) and other male servants employed either within or without the town, except those acting in the capacity of farm-labourers.

"Vakouf" Property.

The conversion of "vakouf" property at the option of the holders into "mulk" (or freehold) property is an expedient by which there is no doubt that the revenue might be very largely increased, and which possesses some singular advantages.

"Vakouf" property is property belonging to the mosques and other religious establishments or benevolent foundations, or in which they are interested, and is administered on their behalf by a special Department of the State called the "Evkaf" Department. It consists of two great classes, viz.: (1) property or its produce actually belonging to such establishments, and held or received on their account by the "Evkaf;" and (2) property owned by private persons, but lapsing, in default of direct* heirs of the owner, to the "Evkaf," and subject in the meantime to a small yearly contribution payable to that Department.

It is to the second of these two classes of "vakouf" property that the proposal for a voluntary conversion into freehold applies. The yearly contribution referred to, originally small in proportion to the value of the property, bears at present a still smaller proportion to it, owing to the greatly diminished value of Turkish currency; and the proposal is based on the well-known fact that a very large number of persons who hold "vakouf" property of this description would willingly pay, as the price of its conversion into freehold, far more than they now pay in their prescribed yearly contribution; so much more, indeed, that the sums which would thus be readily paid would, after supplying the "Evkaf" Department with an amount equivalent to the present yearly payments, and to the reversionary interest in the property which it would lose by the conversion, yield a very large surplus as clear profit to the State.

The amount of revenue which might thus be obtained would undoubtedly be very large; and it seems possible to form some kind of estimate of it by means of the following considerations.

From Returns with which we have been furnished by the "Evkaf" Department, we find that the proceeds of the fixed yearly contributions from "vakouf" property such as that in question amounted in the last year for which the accounts have been made up, to 2,777,748 piastres (or about 22,700*l.*) From the best information which we can obtain

---

* An owner of "vakouf" property having no direct heirs is not debarred from selling it to a person having such heirs, and so preventing it for the time from falling into the "Evkaf."

on the subject, it appears that the rate of these contributions varies from 1 per 10,000 to 1 per 100,000 on the value of the property ; that is to say, their average rate may be taken at 1 per 45,000 on that value. The value, therefore, of the property on which the contributions were paid may be stated at 125,000,000,000 piastres (or 1,000,000,000*l.*) It further appears that the difference in the market value of "vakouf" and "mulk" (freehold property) is from 15 to 30 per cent., or on the average 22½ per cent. If such be the case, an annual payment of ½ per cent. per annum on the value would, there can be little doubt, be willingly made by most owners of "vakouf" property, in return for its conversion into freehold. Now the total value of the property to which the proposed measure would be applicable is (as has been seen) 125,000,000,000 piastres, or 1,000,000,000*l.*, and on this a yearly payment of ½ per cent. would give 625,000,000 piastres, or in round numbers 5,000,000*l.*, which, therefore, would be the gross annual sum realized by the measure, on the supposition that all the owners of this kind of property were to use the power given to them of converting it into freehold.

It is probable, however, that there would be a considerable number of persons, especially among the Mussulman proprietors, who, as much from indifference or dislike to change as from any other cause, would not avail themselves of that power, though we should imagine that such persons would be in a decided minority. Let it be supposed then—a very unfavourable supposition—that no more than one-half of the whole number of proprietors convert their property into freehold, there would still be a gross sum of 2,500,000*l.* (312,500,000 piastres) as the result of the measure. From this must be deducted one-half the sum stated above, 2,777,748 piastres (about 22,200*l.*), as that which is now received in yearly contributions by the "Evkaf" Department; and one-half of the further sum of 4,410,549 piastres (or about 35,300*l.*), which, according to the Returns supplied to us by the Minister of the "Evkaf," has been the average annual amount received during the last nine years on account of "vakouf" property, which has fallen in to the "Evkaf" Department in default of direct heirs : in all, a sum of 3,594,148 piastres (or about 28,750*l.*), which sum would be retained by the "Evkaf" Department, and applied by it to the same purposes as before. It might be desirable, however, to provide that, as regards the converted property there should not only be no loss, but a gain to those interested in the application of the funds derived from "vakouf" sources ; and for this purpose the "Evkaf" Department might be allowed to retain, in each case of conversion into freehold, a sum equal to twice the amount of the yearly contributions which it received from the property before the conversion, besides the proportionate sum payable for the loss of the reversionary interest. On the supposition which we have taken that half the property in question is converted, this (as will be seen) would require the deduction of a further sum of 11,100*l.* from the gross amount. There would remain the sum of 2,460,150*l.*, or 307,518,750 piastres, as clear gain to the State.

We have not been able to discover any valid or even plausible objection to this scheme, which, as we have shown, would benefit all the parties concerned, viz., the State, the holders of the property, and the religious order. We are nevertheless led to believe that there would be much hesitation on the part of the Government to adopt it, owing probably to the ideal aversion entertained by an influential portion of the community to the alienation of "vakouf" property on whatever terms. We have reason to think, however, that if the option proposed to be given were not that of converting the property into freehold, but to allow it to be inherited by near relations, such as a brother or a nephew, there would be no such hesitation. This latter arrangement would of course be less productive to the revenue than the former ; since the payment which the owners would be willing to make in return for the concession would be considerably smaller. Supposing, however, their contribution in the latter case to be ¼ per cent. instead of ½ per cent., there would be still a clear gain to the public treasury of half the amount (2,460,150*l.*) which we have given as the estimated result of the more extended concession, i.e., a clear gain to the Treasury of about 1,200,000*l.*

The advantage to be derived from the proposed measure would not be confined to its direct fiscal value. The increased inducement which would be given to the owners of property to improve its condition, and the additional interest which they would take in it, would contribute not only to the material but to the social welfare of the country.

To these sources of revenue may be added the increase to be expected from the new law respecting stamps, which we should estimate at a sum of at least 50,000*l.*, and which might, if the law were properly administered, be much larger ; from the changes which we have proposed in the tobacco duties, which we should place also at a minimum of 50,000*l.* ; and from the direct collection of the "dîme" in Anatolia, and which, supposing it to produce about the same as it is estimated to yield this year in Roumelia, may be taken at 120,000*l.* The account, therefore, will stand as follows :—

	£		£
Taxation of Constantinople	500,000	Increase on tobacco	50,000
Limited concession to holders of "vacouf" property..	1,200,000	Increase on the "dime" of Anatolia ..	120,000
Tax on domestic servants	450,000	In all	£2,370,000
Increase on stamps	50,000		

Thus showing an increase of revenue which exceeds by 170,000*l.* the sum (2,200,000*l.*) which was required ; and this even on the supposition that the measure respecting " vakouf" property is adopted only in the very modified form which we have indicated as that to which there could be no opposition, and without including any additional sum which it might be possible to raise by means of the optional conversion of " tapou " property into freehold, to which we have referred in a former part of our Report.

We are aware of no obstacle whatever, which the most ordinary courage and energy on the part of the Government might not overcome, to the adoption of these measures. If, however, from some causes which we cannot foresee, any of them should be considered impracticable, there can, it is certain, be little difficulty in supplying their place without any appreciable injury to the industrial and commercial interests of the Empire, or any serious danger of popular discontent.

In this manner, then, the balance-sheet of the Empire may at once be placed in a satisfactory position, supposing that no increase takes place in the present scale of public expenditure ; while the improvements which have already been effected, and those which we trust will be effected, in respect to the taxation of the country and the development of its resources, may be expected, before any long time has elapsed, to increase to a much larger extent the national income, and to place the Porte in a condition, not only to make all due provision for the stability and good government of the Empire in ordinary periods, but to apply in any extraordinary emergency to its own subjects or to foreign nations for a loan at moderate interest without fear of failure.

Public Debt.

A Statement has been furnished to us by the Porte, showing the debts and liabilities of the Ottoman Government. We believe that great care has been bestowed upon the preparation of this Statement ; but owing to the defective mode of keeping the public accounts, full reliance cannot be placed upon its accuracy.

The following is an abstract of the principal items of this account converted into sterling :—

The foreign debt, being in sterling or francs, has been taken at the par of exchange (110 piastres to the 1*l.*), and the remainder at the rate of 125 piastres to the 1*l.*, the rate at which all the general calculations in this Report have been made. It is one of the difficulties experienced in dealing with the Turkish accounts that moneys of different values are mixed up together. Some of the claims are payable in gold, which is at about par ; some in debased silver coin, which is at a discount of from 8 to 10 per cent. ; and the rest in paper, which has varied during the last twelve months between a discount of 20 and 140 per cent. Under these circumstances, and with some prospect that measures will at once be taken for the purpose of diminishing the present large depreciation of the paper currency, the average rate of 125 piastres to the 1*l.* has been thought a not unfair one.

Abstract of Debts and Liabilities of Turkey.

	Currency.	Sterling £.
	Piastres.	
Foreign Debt, at various rates of interest (less sinking funds).. ..	..	14,613,059
Home Debt, viz., stock and bonds :—		
Consolidés, bearing interest at 6 per cent., payable in gold	417,750,000	
Hasné Tahvilis „ „ „ ditto ..	237,500,000	
Sehims, „ „ 8 per cent., payable in paper ..	75,000,000	
Serghis, „ „ 6 per cent., payable in metallic ..	382,104,500	
	1,112,354,500	8,898,836
Debts due by the Finance Ministry, chiefly bearing high interest at various rates, viz.:—		
Borrowed on assignment of revenue	478,902,000	
„ without assignment	41,465,000	
Miscellaneous debts	36,148,995	

	Currency.	Sterling £
	Piastres.	
Sundry liabilities, viz. :—		
War Department ..	66,970,000	
Artillery	13,853,500	
Rediff ..	84,087,000	
Herzegovine	80,611,500	
Syria ..	76,289,704	
Total military	321,811,704	
Admiralty and other naval services ..	80,939,248	
Civil .,	6,476,000	
Civil List	54,117,000	
	463,343,952	3,694,752
Estimated difference of exchange, agio, and interest on payments :—		
In 1276..	59,864,000	
In 1277 .	152,346,500	
	212,210,500	1,697,720
Deficits on budgets :—		
Balance of deficits of 1274 and 1275..	29,043,000	
Deficit of 1276 ..	150,277,065	
Estimated deficit of 1277 ..	212,223,375	
	391,543,440	3,132,348
		36,488,843

From this statement it will be seen that the debt amounts to about 36,500,000*l.*, which in round numbers may be put thus :—

	£
Foreign debt	14,500,000
Home debt, viz., stock and bonds	9,000,000
Debts to Galata merchants and others, at high interest	4,500,000
Claims unpaid, and other Departmental liabilities	8,500,000
Total	£36,500,000

The first two are charged with sinking funds, by which they should be extinguished in the course of twenty or thirty years, while the two latter classes of debts press for immediate settlement, and are the cause of the present financial difficulties of the Turkish Empire.

The sums advanced by the merchants of Galata were principally secured by assignations of the revenue of the past year, but as the bulk of these debts still remains unliquidated, it is evident that the revenue has been applied to other purposes, and, looking to the large deficiency shown upon the Budget of the present year, there does not appear to be much prospect of these claims being met out of the incoming revenue.

The statement of debts is intended, we have been informed, to represent the state of affairs as they will stand at the close of the present financial year, that is, in March next ; and, consequently, the sinking funds payable during the course of the year are deducted from the original amounts.

With regard to the claims and other liabilities they are, as far as we can learn, represented as they existed in March last. At that date power had been taken for the issue of 1,250,000,000 piastres in "caïmé," out of which sum 600,000,000 piastres were specially appropriated, viz. :—

	Piastres.
To proposed Exchange Bank	250,000,000
To replace old "caïmés"	250,000,000
To public works ..	100,000,000
Total	600,000,000

Leaving 650,000,000 piastres available for the payment of claims ; and this amount, it will be seen, has in the Statement been deducted accordingly from the total amount of debts and liabilities. It will, therefore, be observed that the total at the end of the Statement entirely excludes the liabilities of the State on account of the "caïmé" which has been, or is to be, issued, and which (including the capital reserved for the Exchange Bank, which, if not needed for that scheme, will, probably, be used for some other purpose) will amount, at the close of the year, to 1,250,000,000 piastres, and which should properly be added ..

the net sum given in the statement, making, in all, the debts and liabilities of the State amount to 41,500,000*l.* sterling.* The reason given by the Finance Minister for the exclusion of the " caïmé " was that this paper-money being inconvertible and not bearing interest, the State was not bound to repay it at any time, and that, therefore, it need not be looked upon as a liability.

It is, however, to be feared that, with a large deficiency on the budget, and an almost daily fall in the value of paper-money, which adds constantly to the cost of such payments as have to be made in gold or metallic, the amount of liabilities will, before the close of the financial year, be still largely increased, and this consideration makes it most imperative that immediate steps should be taken to add to the means and credit of the State, and to arrest the rapid fall in the value of the circulating medium.

The difficulties in the way of obtaining a loan, either in the country itself or from abroad, sufficient in amount to meet even the most pressing necessities of the State, seem to be such that other resources must be looked to for a palliation of the financial crisis.

The Turkish Government, in its necessities, has largely recourse to the issue of " caïmé," an inconvertible paper, which, although it bears no interest, and is at the present moment at a discount of about 140 per cent., still bears a higher price in the market than do any of the stocks or securities of the Government in this country, although the latter bear high rates of interest and are to be paid off at par within short periods.

For instance, the " consolidés " bearing 6 per cent. interest are now quoted at about 75, purchaseable in paper, which is itself at a discount of nearly 140 per cent., so that 100 piastres " consolidé " can be purchased for about 31 piastres gold, showing a rate of interest of about 19 per cent.

Under these circumstances it is not surprising that the Turkish Government, not clearly seeing the consequences, prefers the issue of paper, which apparently costs it scarcely anything, to the creation of stock, which throws the burden of heavy interest upon the revenue, and that it readily listens to the promises of those who, in return for a handsome contribution from the State, pretend that they can restrain the natural course of monetary transactions, and, by drawing and counter-drawing, change a fictitious and fluctuating into a real and permanent value.

The dangerous effects of the rapid depreciation of the circulating medium, affecting as it does the price of goods and the value of fixed remuneration, and of debts or payments in paper, the uncertainty and risk which it imparts to all the operations of trade, and the vast addition which it makes to the cost of articles which have to be purchased by the Government in gold or metallic, either abroad or in the provinces, creating discontent amongst all classes, and increasing to an enormous extent the public expenditure, as well as the futile and mischievous policy of endeavouring to regulate the exchanges by the interference of the Government, have been so strongly urged upon the Porte that it is to be hoped that the proposed schemes for extending the issue of " caïmé " to the provinces, and for the formation of an establishment to keep up the exchanges by State contributions, will be abandoned.

As regards especially the creation of a Bank of Exchange there could scarcely be a step more fatal to the credit of the State, which it is now absolutely necessary to restore, than the adoption, for the purpose of meeting its difficulties, of a measure contrary to the most elementary principles of political economy, and which actual experience in this country has proved to be powerless for the accomplishment of its object, and disastrous to the interests of the Treasury. The diversion, for the purposes of a fallacious and ruinous scheme, of a sum amounting to 2,000,000*l.* sterling (250,000,000 piastres) which would otherwise be available for the discharge of liabilities imperatively requiring liquidation, is an act to which we trust the Turkish Government does not seriously intend to resort.

The only safe and effective means of meeting the present emergency must be looked for in the determination of the Sultan and his Government to carry out with promptness and with energy the administrative and financial reforms which have been pressed upon their notice.

The debt of Turkey is comparatively speaking so small, and the resources of the country so great, that when once the public confidence is gained there will no longer be any difficulty in obtaining a loan on fair terms, or in consolidating the outstanding liabilities into Government stock.

It will be necessary as soon as possible to establish a surplus of revenue over expen-

							Piastres.
* Net amount given in the Statement	..	..	..	..		..	3,693,384,887
Add "caïmé"..	..	..	..	..	..	..	1,250,000,000
							4,943,384,887

diture. We have indicated certain measures by which, as it seems to us, this object might be the most readily effected, and a sum of 500,000*l*., at the least, obtained, which would be annually available for the purpose of dealing with the debts and liabilities of the State.

In the meantime we would recommend that annuities, either perpetual or for a long term, say 100 years, should be created, and that an effort should be made to induce those who have claims upon the State to accept stock or annuities in lieu of them. It might also be found possible gradually to consolidate a portion of the " caïmé," and to convert the " serghis," " sehims," and other minor securities into this new stock, so as to give it a more important position in the money market, and clear off the minor securities which might interfere with its popularity.

This new stock, in place of being issued at an enormous discount, should bear a high rate of interest, say 12 per cent., and even at this rate of interest it would still have to be issued below par, and thus leave a margin in the price which would act as an attraction to speculators, but would at the same time admit of the prospect that when the credit of Turkey has been re-established, and the stock rises above par, the rate of interest may be reduced.

Certain revenues of the State should be specially assigned as security for the interest of the new stock, and it would add much to public confidence if the revenues of the Empire were paid into a National Bank, founded on a secure and solid basis, and if the public balances were kept at such an establishment in place of at the Treasury, and periodical accounts were published showing the weekly receipts and issues on the public account, and the balances in hand.

There are other means which if properly applied might be made to supply a large amount of ready money, besides adding largely to the prosperity and income of the country.

In place of throwing impediments in the way of the introduction of foreign capital, every means should be taken to encourage foreign enterprise, and to impart to the share-holders of commercial companies a feeling of confidence in the Turkish Government, in the protection which will be afforded them against the opposition of prejudiced officials, and in the even-handed justice that will be administered in cases where their rights are invaded.

Under such circumstances, capitalists and companies would not hesitate to offer high terms for the privilege of working the valuable mines or other resources with which the country abounds, and we have reason to think that if long leases were granted with full security there would not be much difficulty in inserting in the terms of the leases a stipulation that the amount of the first five years' rent should be paid in advance upon the concession being granted ; this measure, if carried out to any considerable extent, would bring large sums of ready money to the coffers of the State, and afford the means of liquidating some of the claims the non-payment of which is so injurious to the public credit.

It may be urged that under the present condition of the country the terms offered would not be so favourable as they might be some years hence when financial order may have been re-established, and roads made ; but it may well be doubted whether owing to this delay bankruptcy may not intervene, and inflict more injury than could be compensated for by any subsequent gain that might be obtained in the terms of the leases ; and the country would in the meantime have lost for several years the great advantages which the advancement of commercial enterprise would afford in the development of the wealth and prosperity of the Empire.

Before concluding our Report it may be well that we should briefly recapitulate the principal remedies which we have suggested for the defects of the Turkish financial system, and for the difficulties to which they have given rise.

We propose then :—

The immediate enlargement of the functions and responsibility of the Minister of Finance, and the reconstruction of his Department in the manner and to the extent which we have described, together with strict regulations for the limitation of the power possessed by the different Departments over the expenditure of public money, and provision for the regular annual publication of the estimates and accounts ;

The reorganization of the " Conseil Suprême du Trésor " by the nomination of members in the place of those who have left it, an addition to the number of its European members, and its recognition and maintenance as an important consultative body, actually responsible for the discharge of the duties entrusted to it, which should be such as we have explained ; ..

The thorough revision of the system under which the public money is accounted for and recorded, and the adoption of the remedies which we have specified, including the creation of an Audit Office for the examination and control of the public accounts, with the aid of a staff of public accountants procured from abroad for that purpose.

With regard to the expenditure, we recommend a reorganization of the public Departments, and of the Naval and Military Services, including the classification of the public servants, a reduction in their number, and a revised scale of salaries and pay; and that means should be taken to render possible the purchase of articles required by the Government at short and fixed dates, instead of at long and uncertain credit.

In order to provide for the immediate equalization of the revenue and expenditure, and to obtain the surplus necessary for enabling the Government to deal with its existing embarrassments, we propose:—

The imposition of a tax in the nature of the " verghi " upon the Capital;

A tax on domestic servants;

An arrangement for the optional conversion of " vakouf " property into " mulk " (freehold), or, if this is not possible, for its transmission, at the option of the holder, to near relations in default of direct heirs;

The adoption, if on consideration it should appear expedient, of a similar course with regard to "tapou " property;

Certain changes in the duties on tobacco;

And an extension of the incidence of the stamp duties, with provision for their more effectual collection.

With a view to the gradual increase of the national resources, so as ultimately to provide a revenue amply sufficient for all the requirements of the State, we recommend, in addition to the improvements which have already been made respecting the collection of the revenue, and the arrangements with foreign Governments with regard to the export and import duties,—

That measures should be adopted for the re-adjustment of the "verghi," as well as of the " rachat militaire;"

That steps should be taken for the gradual substitution, so far as is possible, of direct collection for "farming," as respects the whole of the revenue;

That mines, forests, and other public property should be turned to account, by inviting the free competition of foreign as well as native enterprise, by the substitution of long for annual leases, or by sale in cases where it appears the more profitable course; and especially by allowing foreigners to hold property in their own right, in return for proper reciprocal concessions by foreign Governments;

That interference with the labour of the peasantry by landholders, and with trade and industry by corporations, should cease; and above all, that every effort should be made by the Government to establish roads, and generally to facilitate mercantile traffic and postal intercourse throughout the Empire.

With respect to the debt, we recommend that an endeavour should be made at once to raise the credit of Turkey by the adoption of immediate and energetic measures of financial reform, and by securing a surplus of income over expenditure; that if a loan cannot be obtained to meet the pressing financial difficulties of the State, and to reduce and limit the amount of inconvertible paper, an attempt should be made, by the creation of a stock bearing a high rate of interest, with the best guarantees that can be given for its due payment, to consolidate the various minor classes of Turkish securities, to induce merchants and others to take this stock in payment of their claims, and holders of " caïmé " to convert it into stock at a reasonable rate; and that money should be raised under contracts for leasing mines and Crown properties, to assist in giving effect to these measures.

We also propose the establishment of a National Bank on a sound basis, with branches in the Provinces, through means' of which the financial operations of the Government could be best conducted, and its pecuniary transactions facilitated.

Administrative and Executive improvements of less importance are referred to in the Report; and many others naturally suggest themselves, which have not been touched upon owing to the fear of encumbering more important subjects with too much detail. The principal reforms once effected will, if they are conducted by able and intelligent officers, naturally be followed by the minor changes to which we refer.

It only remains for us to express our confident hope that the Porte will, without further delay, by a prompt, systematic, and comprehensive measure of reform, avail itself of the ample means at its disposal for the re-establishment of its credit and the permanent improvement of its financial condition. The case with which it has to deal is not the hopeless one of a tax-imposing power stretched to its utmost limit, and yet inadequate to meet the demands of a large and inevitable expenditure; but simply of financial disorder, caused chiefly by inattention to the ordinary rules of political economy and fiscal administration. With a taxation, if it were duly adjusted, extremely light; a system of government which, even if made thoroughly efficient in all its branches, would be comparatively inexpensive; and a national debt (including under the term every kind of liability) which is less than 42,000,000*l.* sterling, we cannot believe that the Empire will be permitted any longer to remain in a condition bordering upon insolvency. We have no sufficient reason to suppose that the promise of the new reign will be unfulfilled, or that the Turkish Government, rather than adopt a few simple, obvious, and, with ordinary firmness and prudence, easily feasible reforms, will quietly allow the prevalent predictions of national disaster and decadence to be accomplished.

We have, &c.

(Signed) M. H. FOSTER.
      HOBART.

www.ingramcontent.com/pod-product-compliance
Lightning Source LLC
Chambersburg PA
CBHW021559270326
41931CB00009B/1298